DON'T
SIT ON THE
BABY

The ULTIMATE GUIDE to SANE, SKILLED, and SAFE Babysitting

HALLEY BONDY

Z ZEST BOOKS
MINNEAPOLIS

To my parents, who were my first babysitters. To Tim, my current one. And to Dominik, my favorite little client.

Text copyright © 2022 by Halley Bondy
Illustrations © 2022 by Christian Robinson and Emily Glaubinger

Zest Books™
An imprint of Lerner Publishing Group, Inc.
241 First Avenue North
Minneapolis, MN 55401 USA

For reading levels and more information, look up this title at www.lernerbooks.com.

Visit us at zestbooks.net. 🔵🔵

Main body text set in Janson Text LT Std.
Typeface provided by Linotype AG.

Library of Congress Cataloging-in-Publication Data

Names: Bondy, Halley, 1984– author.
Title: Don't sit on the baby!: the ultimate guide to sane, skilled, and safe babysitting / Halley Bondy.
Other titles: Do not sit on the baby
Description: 2nd edition. | Minneapolis, MN: Zest Books , [2022] | Revised edition of the author's Don't sit on the baby, 2012. | Includes bibliographical references and index. | Audience: Ages 11–18 | Audience: Grades 7–9 | Summary: "Babysitting is one of the most popular jobs for teens, but caring for kids is not easy. Offering useful tips, this funny, updated guide covers basics any babysitting hopeful needs to know and much more"—Provided by publisher.
Identifiers: LCCN 2021057028 (print) | LCCN 2021057029 (ebook) | ISBN 9781728420288 (library binding) | ISBN 9781728420295 (paperback) | ISBN 9781728462714 (ebook
Subjects: LCSH: Babysitting—Vocational guidance—United States—Juvenile literature. | Babysitting—Handbooks, manuals, etc.—Juvenile literature.
Classification: LCC HQ769.5 .B66 2022 (print) | LCC HQ769.5 (ebook) | DDC 649.1/0248—dc23/eng/20211201

LC record available at https://lccn.loc.gov/2021057028
LC ebook record available at https://lccn.loc.gov/2021057029

Manufactured in the United States of America
1-49138-49295-3/14/2022

Contents

Introduction

So you're thinking about babysitting. You love kids, you need the cash, and you have a little free time. Luckily, a fun, entrepreneurial teen like you has tons of opportunities. Even beginners can enter the babysitting force and have plenty of time for school and socializing. It's a great way to build your résumé and earn money for the awesome stuff your parents won't buy—and you get to play hide-and-seek while you're at it!

But all perks aside, babysitting is no cakewalk. After all, if kids weren't a lot of work, sitters wouldn't exist. Children need to be fed, clothed, put to bed, consoled, changed, and most of all, they need to feel safe in your care. As an added challenge, kids can be unpredictable, emotional, and defiant. (Remember all those tantrums you threw as a child? Prepare for swift retribution!) Depending on the kids' ages, the number of children, and their personalities, the pressure can get pretty intense. And when it's all over, you have to wear a smile for the parents—even if you spent an hour scraping macaroni from the ceiling!

With all these demands in your midst, remember that no sitter is perfect. All parents and sitters make mistakes sometimes (they'll be the first to tell you that Mary Poppins doesn't exist!). But if you picked up this book, you're ready to accept the challenge, learn from your mistakes, and accept new, crucial tips.

In the following pages, you'll learn how to deal with the most difficult babysitting experiences. You'll take a quiz to determine what type of babysitting job suits your needs and comfort level. You'll learn the ins and outs of a sitter's responsibilities, from diapers to dinner to bedtime. You'll also learn some babysitting essentials, like how to react in emergency situations, how to play like a kid again, and how to keep a screaming child from driving you up the walls. You'll even read some fun firsthand babysitting stories from teens like you!

On the business side, you'll learn how to set your rate, how to get babysitting jobs, and how to gauge your strengths and weaknesses so you don't feel in over your head. You'll even learn how to take your babysitting expertise to new professional heights.

Most of all, you'll learn how to have fun on the job. You chose this noble profession because kids are the most entertaining, rewarding, and adorable creatures to be around. These little ones need you, and the more prepared you are, the better the job will be for both of you!

Get out there and sit (but never, ever on the baby)!

Halley Bondy

Babysitting Breakdown

1.

What Is Babysitting?

Babysitting is a misleading job title. According to our friends at *Merriam–Webster*, babysitting has nothing to do with sitting on babies. A babysitter is hired to care for children when parents are not home. Babysitting is one of the most popular gigs for teens around. And you can find potential clients in your family, through friends, and in your neighborhood. If you have younger siblings or cousins, you already have experience! And possibly the best part of entering the world of babysitting? It's always an option. As long as there are busy parents in the world, babysitters will have a job caring for their kids.

"Sitting" (as the pros call it) has been around for ages and is a far better job than it used to be. Years ago, in the Victorian era, nannies were typically poor women filling in as parents for rich families. They often started working when they were incredibly young, were treated like servants at best, and spent more time with the kids than the parents did.

But times have changed. These days, nannies tend to watch children for extended hours, such as during the workday, but parents are expected to do most of the heavy lifting themselves and respect childcare workers for all their efforts.

Babysitting is considered different from nannying. Babysitters usually watch kids for a brief period—a few hours, perhaps—while the parents go for a date night, run an errand, or perhaps do some work in another room. This book is specifically for young, beginner babysitters who are balancing school and extracurriculars too.

While babysitting has evolved over the years, the main goal remains the same: to make sure the child stays happy, healthy, and safe in your care. This means making sure they don't watch violent TV shows or gorge on candy and are returned to their parents in one piece at the end of the day or evening. Babysitting is often brushed off as an easy job, but it's not easy, and it's certainly not trivial. Remember, someone's safety is in your hands.

It's a Tough Job

You may have heard that babysitting is easy and that anyone can do it, but that's a myth—babysitting is hard work. Kids fall down. Kitchens catch fire. Parents come home three hours later than they said they would. And sometimes, no matter how much you do to keep the kids happy and entertained, they just won't stop freaking out. How can you do your very best to have fun, keep the peace, and stay calm?

Nobody is born with complete childcare know-how. To babysit, you need skills. Not just basic childcare skills, either. You need patience, intelligence, and a great sense of humor. It takes quick wit to convince Tommy to eat his broccoli. You have a little life in your hands, so everything counts, from your in-control attitude to your negotiating skills, all the way down to your friendly smile.

So, What's in It for You?

Why babysit instead of, say, stock groceries? For one, as a babysitter, you'll have more control over your wages and schedule than other jobs available to you (see "Business Basics"). The arrangement is informal, so you have some flexibility to negotiate. But the rewards go beyond the simple perks. Babysitting can be deeply gratifying. It's a highly creative job. You have to think on your feet and constantly come up with new ways to keep a kid safe and entertained. And not many jobs offer the rush of seeing a toddler walk for the first time or helping a third grader ace a test they were really nervous about. Those are priceless moments, and you won't get those kinds of perks in the produce aisle. Kids often remember their babysitters forever, so think about the impact a babysitter can make on future generations.

2.

What Kind of Sitter Are You?

Love singing nursery rhymes, playing board games, and helping with homework? Then babysitting could be the perfect gig for you. But be warned, not everyone is cut out for childcare. Take this quiz to find out if you really have what it takes.

1. **Your energy level is**
   a. Way too high, I'm told.
   b. I've got a few good hours in me.
   c. Can I get a can of Monster before answering that?

2. **Your niceness level is**
   a. Off the charts.
   b. I'm nice, especially to kids.
   c. I'm sort of nice, until someone annoys me.

3. **Your cleaning habits are**
   a. Persnickety. I can't stand messes.
   b. Moderate. I clean when I must.
   c. What? I don't even notice messes.

4. **You are certified in**
   a. CPR, first aid, Red Cross babysitting classes, or a combination of these.
   b. Nothing, but I have a basic knowledge of CPR, the Heimlich maneuver, and first aid.
   c. R&R. Is there a certificate for that?

5. **Drool and snot are**
   a. Fun!
   b. A part of life.
   c. Totally gross.

6. **Cooking is**
   a. My specialty!
   b. I can use a microwave.
   c. Boring. Takeout for me, thanks.

7. **Your homework helping skills are**
   a. Masterful. l love teaching!
   b. Average. I've helped other kids my age or in my class before.
   c. Nil. I hate explaining things.

8. If you had to pick games to play with a kid, they would be

a. Dolls, kickball, and hide-and-seek.

b. Video games or board games.

c. The quiet game.

9. When an emergency strikes, you

a. Call 911, use my emergency training if applicable, and call the parents.

b. Call the parents.

c. Panic, yell, and hope the whole thing blows over.

10. When you get angry, you

a. Take a few deep breaths and try to approach the problem calmly.

b. Swallow it, smile, and scream when I'm in private.

c. Yell until I get my way.

Find out here what kind of babysitter you are (or aren't):

If you answered mostly As. Are you serious? Nobody likes diapers and drool! Your energy level, patience, and overall childcare smarts make you a natural fit for kids of all ages. With your shining personality and résumé, you'll definitely land a few jobs. However, your passion can be a little overwhelming for some kids and parents. Try to relax sometimes and allow yourself to make mistakes. You're only human!

Mostly Bs. What you lack in professional cred, you make up for in open-mindedness, versatility, common sense, and a can-do attitude. You're eager, capable, and probably ready to hit the job hunt, but it might be better to practice on older kids first. They're (usually) lower maintenance.

Mostly Cs. You may want to consider a different job. Kids get to you easily, and taking care of them is the last thing you want to spend your free time doing. But hey—that's OK. Babysitting is not for everyone.

3.

Types of Jobs to Suit Your Schedule

A neighbor you know very well offers you the baby-sitting gig of your dreams. Responsibilities include watching TV, raiding the fridge, and surfing the web until the parents come home. There's only one kid, and he spends most of his time in his room studying. The job pays, or it might as well, a bajillion dollars an hour. Oh, and you'd get free rein over their swimming pool.

Did somebody say jackpot?! Only . . . there's one teensy issue. It's practically a full-time job. You would need to babysit every day after school for five hours—plus weekends.

Ever an ambitious person, you wrestle with yourself.

Can I squeeze in the time? Maybe if I drop out of swim team, scramble to finish all of my homework on the bus, and study for tests during lunchtime. Or . . . or . . .

Hold it right there, Superman.

Be realistic. There's no way you can sustain a job when you don't have the time. You need to pick the type of job that suits your needs. Unfortunately, this may mean letting a few fantasy jobs slide. It's not a great feeling, but school and extracurricular activities should always come first. Don't worry, another job is always around the corner!

There are several types of babysitting jobs, and each comes with its own set of hours and responsibilities. Below are some of the most common babysitting jobs you'll encounter. Choose wisely!

After-School or Nighttime Sitter

A lot of parents need babysitters between the end of the school day and when they get home from work or when they have evening plans, so after-school and nighttime sitters are in high demand. This kind of job would require some juggling since you likely have your own after-school responsibilities. With this job type, you may have to pick up the kids from school, wait for them at a bus stop, or take them to the park. If they're busy like most kids, they may need an escort to soccer practice or playdates. When the parents are out late, you may have to make dinner and put the kids to bed.

Weekend Sitter

If you're a full-time student—and have, say, volleyball practice every day after school—a weekend babysitting job might be right for you. You wouldn't arrive exhausted after a day of school, and you could still have plenty of time for weekend fun. Like all babysitting jobs, the responsibilities of a weekend sitter depend on the kid's age and needs, but they'll

likely involve prescheduled weekend activities like playdates, soccer games, music lessons, or theater classes. You may need to escort them to and from these events, or if the event calls for it, you may need to be their cheerleader.

Overnight Sitter

Parents go on business trips (or even vacations) without their little ones, so they need someone they can trust to rule the roost overnight. The duties of a part-time overnight sitter include the full range of childcare, from waking kids up in the morning and getting them wherever they need to go to putting them to bed at night (and then maybe doing it all over again the next day). Babysitters who spend the night naturally have to deal with bedtime challenges, like night-mares and bed-wetting, followed by morning chores like preparing breakfast. Overnight sitters should have some extra emergency training, since they're watching the kids (and the house and any pets) for such a huge chunk of time. It's a big responsibility, so parents will usually hire experienced sitters or sitters they know very well for these positions.

Summer Sitter

If you don't want to sit on the couch this summer, it might be a great time to babysit! If your schedule is wide open, you could use the time to earn lots of cash (and add some points on your résumé). Since most parents still have to work, there is a wide range of need for babysitters, from a few hours to a few times a week. Sometimes families bring highly trusted babysitters along for trips, which could mean a trip to the beach for you! It could also mean watching over the kid in an unfamiliar environment, so summer sitters should be confident and adaptable.

With so many kinds of babysitting jobs out there, there's sure to be one that's right for you. Be realistic with yourself about your schedule and abilities, and you'll find your match!

4.

What to Expect from Kids Ten and Under

Kids come in a variety of ages, and each age requires a different level and type of care. As a babysitter, you'll need to decide what age group you're most comfortable with so that you can narrow down your job hunt. Not sure? This quick breakdown will clue you in on the personality traits and skills you'll need to care for kids up to the age of ten.

Newborns (Up to 3 Months Old)

WHAT THEY'RE LIKE

- These tiny creatures can hardly move or support their own heads.
- They need a good dose of formula or pumped breast milk about every two to four hours.

- Newborns sleep for fourteen to seventeen hours a day at two- to three-hour intervals.
- Newborns need their diapers changed frequently.

- A gentle touch and a desire to be really needed. Newborns are fragile (their bones haven't fully developed yet), and you'll be carrying them a lot.
- Decoding skills. Cracking the newborn language code isn't easy. They don't cry only when they're hungry. Maybe the little booger already ate and needs to be burped. Or maybe they're uncomfortable and need a diaper change, an extra sweater, or a good rocking session. It's your job to figure it out.
- Maturity. In general, you shouldn't babysit for a newborn until you're older and have plenty of experience.

Infants (4–11 Months Old)

WHAT THEY'RE LIKE

- These kids are starting to crawl, sit, and eventually walk (with your help!).
- Younger infants are probably learning how to hold their own bottles, while older ones are likely eating mushy stuff (like baby food) on top of their scheduled feedings.

If they can support their own heads and necks, they can sit in a high chair during meals.

- Diapers are still the norm.
- Infants usually sleep multiple times a day for a couple of hours or less at a time.
- An infant's "talk" may help you figure out why they're crying.
- Infants start teething at six months old, so there may be some drooling and crankiness.
- They also start to feel separation anxiety at about nine months old, which means they may need extra support and attention after their parents leave.

WHAT YOU'LL NEED

- A cautious eye to make sure that the kids don't sidle up next to sharp things, like scissors or table corners.
- Plenty of cleaning materials nearby for the food and drool.
- A patient attitude.
- The ability to have fun with stuffed animals, reading, finger puppets, and more.

Toddlers (1–2 Years Old)

WHAT THEY'RE LIKE

- These kids can move. Fast. This can be challenging in the middle of a diaper change or dinner, or when safety hazards (like stairs) are involved, but they will give you a great workout!

- Toddlers can usually drink out of covered cups and eat solid food with their hands.
- They sleep for about ten to twelve hours at night and one or two hours during the day.
- They'll likely still need diapers, though some early birds start potty training at this age.
- They should be able to tell you (even if it's in their own special language) that they need to be changed.
- There's a reason they call it the terrible twos. They are very expressive with their feelings, happy or not!

WHAT YOU'LL NEED

- A lot of patience. These kids want to assert their independence, and sometimes the best way they know how to do that is with a tantrum. The ability to take a deep breath, use a calm tone of voice, and solve problems creatively is crucial.
- Lots of extra energy and ideas, since these kids are starting to get into active games like tag or finding hidden objects.

Preschoolers (3–4 Years Old)

WHAT THEY'RE LIKE

- Preschoolers can walk and run on their own, though they'll need to hold your hand sometimes, especially when crossing the street.

- By this age, kids are typically potty training with adult assistance, and they may wear diapers at night or have some instances of bed-wetting.

- These kids need supervision in the tub, and they probably need help getting cleaned and dressed.
- These kids can tell you when they're hungry and what they want to eat, and they are learning to feed themselves with regular utensils. (But they can be picky eaters!)
- Some of these kids will do anything to get out of bedtime, and when they do go to sleep, they may have nightmares!

WHAT YOU'LL NEED

- A lot of creativity (and maybe your old Halloween costumes). Preschoolers love make-believe games. They also love books, and they're just learning the basics of reading.
- Patience and love. They are exploring their world with quite a lot of energy, and sometimes they make mistakes or have emotional reactions. They may need a little TLC and flexibility.
- An arsenal of lullabies. While they sleep for about ten to twelve hours at night, four-year-olds may have trouble falling or staying asleep.

Kindergarteners to Second Graders (5–7 Years Old)

- My, my, they grow up so fast! These kids can pretty much take care of the basics—dressing, eating, and bathing—by themselves, so you probably won't need to chase them down too much. Unless, of course, you're playing tag.
- They may still need help with more advanced tasks like cutting, drawing, and reading, but that's the fun part.
- Kindergarteners may still be picky about what food they eat, but they can eat regular meals without your help (and they probably don't want your help either).
- They should be able to go to the bathroom and take a bath without your help (though you should always supervise bath time).
- At night, there might be some rare cases of bed-wetting.

- Stellar negotiating tactics. By now kids can speak clearly, and they've also learned how to use words to their advantage.
- Creative cooking skills. Kids this age tend to be picky eaters.
- A love of board games, creative play, sports, and more.

Third to Fifth Graders (8–10 Years Old)

- These kids are more or less independent and biding time before they don't need a babysitter.
- You'll probably still need to cook or order food for them, but they can at least help around the kitchen.
- If you do need to chase them down for anything, it will likely be to do their homework (which they might need your help with). Better brush up on that long division!

- They're pretty much up to their own thing, so you'll need to figure out when to stay out of their way (for example, if they have a trusted friend over and they'd like to play a game without you—of course you'll still be keeping an eye on them) and when to intervene (such as if they're online when they're not supposed to be).
- An ability to set boundaries. Even though you are closer in age, you are their sitter, not their bestie.

Kids with Disabilities

Some children have disabilities that require additional or alternative care. For example, a child with autism may be hypersensitive to certain fabrics and so avoids wearing clothing made with those materials. A child who uses a wheelchair may need to take an alternate, accessible route to a park or to school. Or a child with dyslexia may need you to help them read instructions on a homework assignment. Kids with disabilities are like everyone else—they need to feel included and cared for. Talk to parents about any special accommodations their children may need before your first day on the job so that you have all the information you need to make sure things go smoothly for you and for the kids. Chances are, parents will only hire older, experienced caregivers to watch over a child with a severe disability. If you're interested in learning more about disability, start by reading books like *The Disability Experience* by Hannalora Leavitt or *We Should Hang Out Sometime* by Josh Sundquist.

5.

Getting Started

So, you've taken a quiz, worked out how many free hours you have in your schedule, and mulled over your tolerance for diapers. You're pretty confident in your babysitting skills. But do you really have what it takes? Maybe, but you don't want to test your new knowledge after the parents leave you alone with three kids!

If you walk into a babysitting job cold, you may be overwhelmed by surprises. Maybe you've never experienced how much attention they truly need or how challenging it can be to hold a baby and keep a home reasonably clean. The hard reality of babysitting is a lot different from running through scenarios in a book.

So before you start a babysitting job, practice on some real live kids in a less urgent environment. Get to know them. Test your game skills, your tantrum strategies, your homework help, your cooking abilities—whatever you think may be challenging on the job.

But where do you find your guinea pigs? Keep reading. (If you already have experience with children, feel free to skip to the next chapter!)

Go for the sibling. You may have a little brother or sister. Then you know perfectly well what a handful little kids can be. But you could still improve your babysitting skills by helping your parents with the rough stuff once in a while. Volunteer to cook dinner for your little sister tonight. Try introducing new games into the fold. If she starts throwing a minor fit, try resolving the issue without getting Mom (as long as it's safe). These are all skills that you need in a baby-sitting situation, so why not start at home?

Talk to neighbors, family friends, or relatives. You could ask trusted relatives or friends to let you hang around their kids (with their parents around) for experience. If you go to the movies with your family, for example, you can practice things like escorting the kids to the bathroom or buckling them in a car seat on the way home. Parents might be grateful for the help!

Babysit while parents are home. Some parents need babysitters while they're still in the house. Maybe they work from home, or maybe they just need an extra hand. Whatever the reason, this can be a great way to gain experience and maybe even make some money.

Volunteer. You don't have to go to a house to get experience with kids. You can also volunteer at local schools, summer camps, religious centers, libraries, museums, day-care centers, or neighborhood associations—you get the picture. Often these kinds of institutions take young volunteers to help run events like block parties or field trips.

Get a mentor. Do you know somebody who has some babysitting experience? Don't be afraid to ask them for advice. After all, they were once in your shoes.

Essential Skills

6.

Feeding Hungry Mouths

It seems so simple. Food goes in mouth. Mouth chews food. Food gets swallowed. The end. Right? So, why is Laila using her macaroni as a telescope? And what do you do if she cries when the vegetables touch the meat? And on what planet are gummy bears a meal?

These questions have been confounding adults the world over. Some kids are puzzling eaters. But while it's not worth probing the logic behind macaroni as an astronomic tool, as a babysitter, you still have to ensure that your young charges eat.

During meals, you may have to cook, clean, and work around children's tastes as well as their food sensitivities. Food requirements will vary depending on the ages of the children (see page 19) and the time of day that you babysit (see page 15). The next few pages include tips to help make mealtimes easier. Remember, you should

always get the full rundown from the parents on dietary restrictions (they may be a vegetarian household, or have a child with a peanut or other food allergy) and any religious or cultural customs (think chopsticks instead of knives and forks, or maybe it's Ramadan, Passover, or Lent).

Bottle-Feeding Basics

If you're babysitting for infants or toddlers, you'll probably use baby bottles. Giving a baby a bottle may seem like an easy, two-step process: you fill the bottle and feed the kid. But there are a number of things to think about, like what to put in the bottle, what temperature the liquid should be, and how to hold the baby so they don't choke. While older infants and toddlers may be able to feed themselves (with a little help from you), a little baby is way too young to hold a bottle on their own. Below are some best practices you can employ to ensure a successful feeding session.

1. **Ask if everything is sterilized.** Bottles, bottle nipples, caps, and rings need to be squeaky clean. Otherwise, the baby can get sick from germs. Often, parents will have already sanitized everything before they head out the door—but it's good to know what to do if you find yourself without a clean bottle. If the bottles and accessories are new, boil them in water for five minutes and cool them completely before you use them. If they've been used before, wash them in a clean basin with soap, water, and a clean bottle brush. You don't want to wash

bottles in the sink, as it may contain germs that could contaminate the bottles. And don't forget to wash your hands!

2. **Fill the bottle.** Bottles can be filled with pumped breast milk or baby formula, depending on the age of the child and the feeding preferences of the parents. A parent should have already given you specific instructions, but here are some additional pointers for each liquid:

a. **Breast milk.** Refrigerated breast milk goes bad after four days, while frozen breast milk goes bad after about six months. Most moms will have dates on the bottles, so check those and use the older—but not expired—ones first. Some parents are extra careful about contamination, and they'll ask you to throw away any leftover breast milk after one feeding. If not, store the leftover breast milk in the fridge between feeding times.

b. **Baby formula.** You may have to mix powdered formula with water (the water should be from a safe source of drinking water—usually tap water is safe, but a parent may ask you to use bottled or filtered water instead), or the drink may be ready-made. Follow the instructions on the packaging, and strictly abide by the expiration date.

Ready-made formula usually stays edible for forty-eight hours after opening as long as it's stored in the fridge. You shouldn't store powdered formula after it has been mixed as it may get clumpy.

3. **Test the temperature.** If the parents tell you to warm the milk or formula before feeding, you can't just pop it in the microwave or warm it up on a stove. You'll burn the kid's mouth, and you may even change the chemicals in the food. Instead, fill the bottle with the liquid food and run it under a warm tap. Shake it well, and test the temperature by putting a drop on the back of your hand. The drop should be close to room temperature, and it shouldn't leave a pink mark on your hand. If it does, it's still too hot!

4. **Prep the baby.** Attach a clean bib around the baby's neck. Have a clean, soft cloth handy to wipe up any messes. Hold the bottle with one hand, and hold the baby close to you with the other. (They should be in a slightly upright position, with their head higher than their body.) Make sure both you and the baby are comfortable, because you could be in this position for a while.

5. **Start the bottle-feeding.** Hold the bottle upside down until the nipple fills with milk. You want the baby to swallow as little air as possible, or you'll pay for it during burp time when they let out a stinky, milky belch. Tap the tip of the nipple against the baby's lips. They should respond by putting it in their mouth. As the baby sucks on the bottle, look for little bubbles rising from the nipple. If you don't

see bubbles, the milk may not be flowing out. Make sure that the nipple isn't clogged or that the nipple hasn't collapsed (that is, sucked in toward the bottle). Both of these problems may be helped by loosening the top slightly.

6. **Look for spit-up.** Spit-up is a cute way of saying "a little puke." Babies' digestive systems aren't fully developed yet, so they'll spit up after they eat. This is totally normal. Just use the cloth to wipe up the baby's mouth. You should only be concerned if they projectile vomit, or they vomit brown or green, which could be bile or blood, not milk. If this happens, call the parents immediately.

7. **Take a burp break.** Swallowing air is an unavoidable part of bottle-feeding. And it can be pretty irritating for an infant. (It can also increase their spit-up.) This is why it's important to burp a baby after they drink about 2 to 3 ounces (59 to 89 mL). When you burp a child, hold them close to your chest while supporting their neck with one hand and letting their chin rest on your shoulder. Repeatedly pat their back gently until they let out a nice, healthy belch. Some babies may need a firmer pat than others. Just make sure that you've got a towel under their chin or on your shoulder to catch any surprise spit-up.

8. **Know when to stop.** The baby may be finished (or may be taking a break) when they close their mouth, stop sucking, or turn away from the nipple. If you already burped them and they don't continue eating, they're probably full. But if they reject food for hours, there may be a problem, so inform the parents immediately.

Baby Food Rules

Baby food is like grown-up food, only a lot mushier. Most kids can start eating baby food when they're between four and six months old, though it's really up to the parents. Some parents will want you to give their kids baby food in addition to breast milk or formula in bottles or covered sippy cups. Others may tell you to stick to baby food alone. If parents prefer homemade concoctions like mashed-up rice cereal or puréed vegetables, meat, and fruit versus ready-to-eat baby food from a jar, they should prepare it for you. Or make sure they give you thorough instructions on how to cook and store the food so you can prep it yourself. Ready to eat? Here are some quick tips to get you started:

- **Prep for mealtime.** Just as with bottle-feeding, you want to wash your hands and put a bib on the kid. If they're old enough to sit in a high chair, you want to make sure they're buckled securely in place. (Don't use a high chair until the parents show you how.) You can also spoon-feed the child while holding them upright on your lap. Make sure you have a clean cloth handy!

- **Let them play.** Children may attempt to eat with their hands. This is normal. They may want to hurl their food around or use it as a toy. If they're still discovering finger food, you should tolerate the play. You can try to cajole them into taking an occasional bite by pretending to eat it too or by doing an "airplane" move into their mouths.

SAFETY FIRST

Q. What do I do if a child is choking?

A. It's important to get certified in proper first aid before babysitting. Instructors will run through a variety of scenarios like this so that you know what to do when disaster strikes.

    If a child aged one year or older is choking (meaning they swallowed something and they can't cough, breathe, or make noise), you should perform the Heimlich maneuver. Do the following:

1. Kneel behind the child, wrap your arms around their waist, and place the thumb part of your fist against the child's stomach, between their navel and their sternum.

2. Wrap your other hand around your fist, and thrust quickly in an inward, upward motion. Be gentle with little kids.

3. Thrust until the food pops out of their mouth, or until they faint. If they faint, call 911. Check to see if they are breathing and have a pulse. If not, and you are certified, you should start performing CPR (see page 76 to find out how).

If the child is less than a year old:

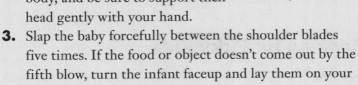

1. Place the baby facedown on your forearm, using your thigh for support.

2. Hold their head lower than their body, and be sure to support their head gently with your hand.

3. Slap the baby forcefully between the shoulder blades five times. If the food or object doesn't come out by the fifth blow, turn the infant faceup and lay them on your lap to keep their head supported.

4. Place two fingers on the middle of their breastbone, and give five quick thrusts down, compressing the chest, but not too hard.

5. Alternate between the back slaps and chest thrusts until the object comes out. If the baby becomes unconscious, call 911 after two minutes of infant CPR (see page 76 to find out about CPR and certification). If you're able to see the object in their throat, you may be able to remove it with your finger, but only do this if it's in plain sight.*

If you are ever in doubt about what to do or how to do it, ask the 911 dispatcher.

---

* Instructions taken from the 2020 American Heart Association Guidelines for Cardiopulmonary Resuscitation and Emergency Cardiovascular Care, part 4, section 17.2.

- **Accept the mess.** Food that falls on the floor is a lost cause and a natural part of baby feeding. The same with all those dribbles on the bib. However, you may be able to save the food that winds up on a baby's chin and lips. Just scrape the stray food with a baby-friendly rubber-covered spoon, pretend the spoon is an airplane, and put it into their mouth. Clean up the food bits after.

Cooking for Picky Kids

Some kids love simple foods like sandwiches, but if you don't cut them diagonally, they may refuse to eat them. Other kids may initially refuse vegetables. It's not an insult to your culinary genius. Pickiness is a natural, random phenomenon that generations of babysitters have weathered. If a kid throws their food on the floor, don't take it personally. Instead, follow these tips:

1. **Stick to the parents' routine.** Try not to introduce new food to picky eaters right away. It's better to stick to the parents' menu. Once you get accustomed to the kid, you can start being more spontaneous. Until then, keep that tuna-cheese-celery surprise (or any surprise) on the back burner.

2. **Make food awesome.** Food looks a lot more interesting when it's in the shape of a smiley face, when it's part of a theme night (orange-colored dinner night?), or when you accompany every successful bite with a funny song. Make healthy food appealing by adding a kid-friendly touch (yogurt with sprinkles, anyone?). Turn to pages 42 and 44 for two awesome recipe ideas.

3. **Avoid bribing.** A lot of people haggle with kids to make them eat. A common tactic is saying, "Eat five more string beans and you'll get dessert," or, "Drink your milk and then you can play video games." These seem like reasonable trades, but experts don't recommend this kind of bribery. Children will start to see food as one big power struggle. Try asking the parents for their secrets.

4. **Get rid of distractions.** Sometimes kids will decline food, not because they're full but because they've got one eye on the cartoons in the next room. Before mealtime, turn off the TV and put away the toys so the kids can focus on eating.

5. **Let their appetite speak.** Kids know when they're hungry, and they know when they're full. You don't want to force-feed kids, you don't want to rush them, and you don't want to pressure them to make sure they eat every crumb. Your job is to make sure that the kids eat enough healthy food to tide them over until their parents come home. This is a lot easier if you pay attention to the kids' actual hunger levels. If they're still just not eating, try another tactic on this list.

6. **Eat with the kids.** This makes eating more of a bonding experience for the kids instead of a lonely chore. It may also encourage them to eat. They may take your example and try to imitate your impressive fork skills.

7. **Let them help.** Children are more likely to enjoy meal-time if they have a part in it. If they're old enough, allow the kids to help you cook, set the table, or wash dishes, and then praise them for a job well done. Obviously, never let a child handle boiling water, scalding surfaces, or sharp knives on your watch. The point is to make mealtime a fun bonding experience.

Here are two easy recipes that are sure to please many kids:

ANTS ON A LOG (for Children Ages Two and Up)

It may have the least appetizing name in the world, but ants on a log is a timeless, delicious treat. It's also easy to make and healthy.

You Need
- a handful of celery stalks
- peanut butter
- 4 to 5 raisins per stalk

Rinse the celery stalks, and then cut the ends off so that there is a U-shape on both ends. Cut the stalks lengthwise into skinny strips (full sticks can be a choking hazard!). Let the kids use a spoon to fill the celery stalk with peanut butter. Once the whole celery stalk is full, they can apply raisins along the peanut butter—like ants crawling on a log. Alternative fillings could be almond butter, sunflower butter, hummus, cottage cheese, or cream cheese. Alternative ants could be pieces of pear or carrots, sunflower seeds, or dried cranberries.

TALES FROM THE CRIB

I remember a time when I was babysitting for my seven-year-old younger brother and he complained of being hungry. I had no idea what to make him, but I had a lot of bravado. So, I asked, "Do you want something out of the box or a can?" He told me he wanted a sandwich. OK, easy enough! I then asked, "Do you want ham? Do you want jelly?" He wrinkled his nose and said, "Jelly is gross!" I asked, "How about tuna?" He said, "Fish is icky!" (Mind you, he had never tried fish in his life.) We went back and forth a few more times before he said, "I want peanut butter." Then we had to decide what kind of peanut butter: smooth or chunky. When we got to the bread, he said he wanted it cut into triangles. Finally, I was done: I had chunky peanut butter on triangle-shaped bread—a forty-minute adventure!

—Jessie G., fifteen

No, they don't just exist in the Dr. Seuss book. You can actually make this delightful delicacy with the power of eggs, ham, and magic (or food coloring).

You Need

- ½ to 1 slice of ham
- 2 eggs
- 1 teaspoon of milk
- green food coloring
- 1 tablespoon butter or olive oil

First, cook the ham (without the help of the children). To do this, turn the stove on low. Add half the butter or olive oil in a frying pan. Put the ham in the pan, and wait until the slices become slightly crispy (but not burned) on both sides. When you think the ham is done, turn off the stove and set the ham aside. Cook the eggs. Let the kids try cracking all the eggs into a big bowl (teach them how to avoid getting egg shells in the food!). Have them beat the eggs with a fork or whisk until the liquid is all yellow. Add the milk. Ask the kids to add a few drops of green food coloring to the egg batter while you (or another sibling) continue beating it. Watch them stare in awe as the egg batter turns green! Set the food dye aside, and ask the children to step away from the stove. Turn on the stove. Add the remaining butter or oil to a frying pan, and pour in the eggs. Move the eggs around the pan with a spatula until there's no more liquid egg left. The eggs should be the consistency of mashed potatoes: not too runny, not too hard. Place the ham next to the eggs on a plate, and *voila*! You've made Dr. Seuss proud.

7.

Dealing with Diapers and Potties

You have a nine-month-old baby on your lap, and things start to stink. (Didn't you just change her?) Knowing full well that unmentionable things are happening on your jeans, you rush to the diaper changing table, wipes at the ready. But when you open the diaper, it's totally clean. Relieved but baffled, you return to the couch.

Five minutes later, the stench picks up again. Once more, you run to the changing table. Clean diaper. And again. Clean diaper. You sit back down and crank up the TV volume. The stink intensifies, but by now you've learned your lesson. You don't budge. And of course, that's when the unmentionable *really* happens. Worse, by now, the diaper is so loose from all that fastening and unfastening, it couldn't contain the avalanche. You, babysitter, like so many babysitters before you, are covered in poop.

Diapers and toilet training are stinky realities of baby-sitting little kids. Until they are fully potty-trained, you have to do a lot of the dirty work for them, and sometimes it can be a bit of a guessing game. It's best to just accept the challenge.

Changing Diapers

Babies eat all the time, so they poop and pee all the time too. You can usually tell it's time for a diaper change by the stench. But as the scenario above shows, the baby may just be fussy and gassy—also, very little babies who only eat breast milk don't  have stinky poop. If it's been about two to three hours since their last diaper change, you'll want to take a peek. Toddlers may even be able to tell you they need a diaper cleanup. When the time comes, wash your hands, and then follow these simple instructions:

1. Prepare everything you need. Before the parents leave, find out where everything is. You'll need baby wipes; clean diapers; diaper rash cream; a soft, clean cloth for the baby to lie on; dirty clothes storage and handling; and, if necessary, a change of clothes for the baby.

2. Most parents use a specific changing table where they stock all their supplies. Lay the baby on their back on a changing table or other designated clean, flat surface.

(Never leave a baby unsupervised. They could roll over and fall.)

3. Remove the baby's bottom clothes and the dirty diaper. Most diapers have tabs on both sides that stick together (though cloth diapers often have buttons). Peel off each tab, lift the baby's legs with one hand, and slide the dirty diaper out with the other hand.

4. Throw the dirty diaper away in the diaper bin or, if there is none, the trash can. (Make sure you don't toss it in the family laundry hamper by accident.) If the parents use cloth diapers, ask them how they handle poop.

5. Lift the child's legs again, and use baby wipes to clean their bottom and privates. (Always wipe from front to back.) Throw away the dirty diaper wipes before you move on.

6. Grab the clean diaper and open it. Lift the baby by the legs again and slide the diaper under their butt. The wider side (where the sticky tabs are) should be on the bottom.

7. Latch the front and back of the diaper together with the sticky tabs on the sides. Make sure the diaper is on securely to avoid any avalanches! Put the baby's clothes on, and you're done. Don't forget to wash your hands again!

SAFETY FIRST!

Q: How do I deal with and avoid diaper rash?

A: Diaper rash is an irritation of any skin covered by the diaper, often caused by buildups of bacteria or yeast that love moist environments like babies' diapers. You can tell when a baby has diaper rash by big red splotches and inflamed scaly skin anywhere on the skin inside the diaper. It's easy to treat by applying cream to the infected area, but if diaper rash gets too out of control, it can lead to a more serious infection. Ask the parents what cream (if any) you should use. To prevent diaper rash, you should keep the area as dry as you can. Change their diapers every two to three hours. Wrap the diaper loosely so there's air traveling inside, and don't use any harsh soaps when you wash the child.

Potty Training

Believe it or not, toilets can be trickier than diapers. Diapers offer a nice safeguard against disasters, but kids who are just learning how to use a toilet can have accidents at any time. Parents should not use an untrained babysitter when the kids are first starting out with potty training. But if the kids are pretty far along and just need some help, you can minimize mishaps by gently encouraging them to go to the bathroom as much as possible, especially before they leave the house, after every meal, and before they go to bed. If you spot them clutching their pants, fidgeting, or just looking really uncomfortable, know that those

are telltale signs that they have to use the toilet. Here's what to do when you get there:

1. Put a potty-training seat on the toilet bowl if necessary. This is a small booster seat that saves the kid from falling into the toilet. Sometimes, kids may even use miniature potties while they train. Make sure you ask the parents where these magical training tools are before they leave.

2. If you're at a public toilet, be sure to use a disposable toilet cover (or two) to give the little one a clean place to sit.

3. Unfasten the child's pants and underpants if they need help.

4. Explain what you're doing so they can learn the steps to do it themselves. Remember, potty training is a learning experience and *you* are the teacher.

5. If the child is too small to get onto the toilet seat themselves, help lift them. They may also need to hang on to your arm for support.

TALES FROM THE CRIB

It's difficult to predict what will happen while you're babysitting. Whether it's an incident involving learning to share or fussiness over a meal—we must always expect the unexpected and prepare ourselves to control any situation that may occur.

One thing I was definitely not expecting was to find myself listening to four-year-old Lauren talk about her boyfriend, Jack. She smiled while recounting how they play on the monkey bars together and told me the story of when he asked her to marry him (they were going down the slide—how romantic!).

She looked at me, puzzled, as I was laughing along, and I realized how sure of her love she was. That's one of the best parts of babysitting, though—getting to know the kids you're with and watching them over time as they mature and grow. I love sitting for kids who are young enough to believe in fairy tales and Santa Claus because they have active, developing imaginations not yet tainted by society. That definitely describes Lauren, and I just hope that I'm invited to the wedding!

—Audrey, fourteen

6. Wipe the child with toilet paper or baby wipes before refastening their clothes. (Always wipe from front to back.)

7. Have the child wash their hands with you. You can tell them they're done washing after they sing "Happy Birthday" twice.

Then congratulate them for completing a successful potty-training session.

What to Do When Accidents Happen

Despite your best efforts, kids will pee in their pants sometimes. It's not fun to deal with, but it's important to stay positive throughout the child's potty-training days, even when they make mistakes. Here's how you can handle accidents like a pro:

1. Always be prepared. Never leave the house without clean underwear or clean diapers, baby wipes, a fresh pair of clothes, and some plastic bags. Some parents may already have this stuff prepared in a backpack.

2. Even if an accident happens in public, don't make a big deal out of it. And don't make them feel bad. Instead, say, "Good try!" "It's okay," or "We'll fix it."

3. Bring the child to the nearest bathroom or private area. Sometimes it helps to plan ahead for this—for example, only bring the child to restaurants and stores with large bathroom areas.

4. Remove any soiled clothes, and put them in a plastic bag if you're in public or the appropriate laundry receptacle if you're at home.

5. Wipe the kid down with baby wipes, and put fresh underwear and clothes on them. If absolutely necessary, put on a diaper, especially if they have had a few mishaps already—parents will understand if it's just one of those days. Then wash your hands!

8.

Getting Kids Dressed

Making sure kids are properly clothed is often an important part of a babysitter's to-do list. Babies need your help getting their arms and legs into onesies. Some two-year-olds have only one pair of shoes they like. Most kids can't dress themselves without you until they're about four years old!

Imagine you're babysitting for a very fashionable little kid, which is thrilling because you too are a stylista. When it's time to choose her outfit for the day, you furiously comb the drawers for the cutest stuff you can find. Purple tights, yes! Green jumper, yes! Orange cowboy hat, obviously! By the end of this ordeal, she looks like a 3-foot-tall (0.9 m) kaleidoscope, and it's *soooo cuuuute*!!!

And then buzzkill hits. It's Saturday. She has soccer practice. And it just rained all over the turf—which means a lot of mud. Then you realize you have to leave in five minutes.

You beg. You plead. You fight. But this blinding rainbow child is just not getting into shin guards now.

You should be prepared to help little ones change into everything from school clothes to pajamas to sports uniforms. While there's no way to make dressing time go perfectly every day, there are ways to expedite it, and crazy-color dress-up time right before soccer practice probably isn't one of them!

1. **Ask for instructions.** Kids have different wardrobe requirements depending on their age, their clothing preferences, and what their parents want them to wear. Parents know best. They even know better than the chicest, opinionated kids, so be sure to ask your bosses what the deal is before you let the kids go wild. Here are some questions you'll want to ask:

   - Can the child dress themselves? What kind of help do they need?
   - Where do you keep the socks, shoes, shirts, pants—(you get the idea)?
   - Where do you put dirty clothes?
   - Do they have to wear a school uniform?
   - Do they require a sports uniform or any other equipment for scheduled activities?
   - If the child has a disability, are there any considerations I should take when I put clothes on or take them off?

SAFETY FIRST

Q. *How do I dress babies safely?*

A. *Between spit-up and overflowing diapers, babies need their outfits changed pretty often to stay clean and sanitary. When you change an infant's clothes, you need to keep their head supported and choose loose clothes that won't suffocate them. Onesies with snaps are the easiest outfits to maneuver, so opt for these if you can. That way, you can open the onesie on a table and lay the baby on top of it. Gently move their arms and legs into the outfit and snap it closed. Ideally, they should have a fresh diaper too. (See page 45 for more on diapers.)*

2. **Plan ahead.** Rushing may agitate kids, decreasing your chances of success. Give yourself plenty of time to dress them. Factor in potential delays, like having to chase little ones around the house or having to find their black shoes because who knows where they are. Also, plot some smooth moves to save time, such as untying and loosening shoes before asking kids to put them on.

3. **Make it a joint effort.** Toddlers and older kids will like dressing more if you involve them in it. For example, one-year-olds can probably remove their own socks, and preschoolers may want to pick their own shirt or pants. Make the socks into cute little monsters that want to eat their feet. Ultimately, encouraging children to dress themselves will teach them to be more independent.

4. **Check for pitfalls.** You don't want any clothing safety hazards on your hands. Before letting kids loose in their new outfits, check that their pants aren't too long and make sure their shoes are on nice and tight. Oh, and don't let them run around on hard floors in their socks. That's a big slip just waiting to happen.

9.

Playtime

So you're relatively new at a babysitting gig, and you want to make a fun first impression. You buy My Little Pony figures to surprise the twin girls before bedtime. After all, My Little Pony was totally your thing when you were their age. They're going to *love* them.

But when you open those glorious, nostalgic pink boxes, the kids couldn't care less about the rainbow horsie manes and brushes. Instead, they run to the den and invent a game of their own—one that involves a giant pillow fort that Godzilla (you) must destroy at all costs.

Why Godzilla, of all things? you think. *You can braid Twilight Sparkle's hair! And how do these kids know about 1950s Japanese horror flicks anyway?*

Face it, sitter: My Little Pony is not on the menu tonight.

Kids' playtime preferences can be totally unpredictable. Nobody holds the secret to pleasing every kid right away. So even if you have a really cool plan, remember that it may not go the way you want. Let things happen as they will. There's nothing wrong with My Little Pony, but these kids just aren't into it. Move on. Embrace your new Godzilla identity. And be creative with it: Godzilla could have a British accent or wear a shoe on their head. The possibilities are endless.

Structuring Play by Age

Every kid is different. If you had to tattoo one babysitting rule on your forehead, it would be that. But even so, kids in certain age groups have certain preferences. You wouldn't give an eight-year-old a baby rattle or try to play board games with a newborn, right? Taking kids' ages into consideration will make life a lot easier for them and for you. Here are the general age groups and what each one is into:

BIRTH TO NINE MONTHS

For babies, playtime and any other time of day (like bedtime or snack time) are not much different. Playtime never really ends for them, and everything's a kind of game. And even though babies don't exactly do much, there are lots of ways to play with them. They get a kick out of cool sounds, soft touches, being lifted into the air, playing peekaboo, and just watching you mess around with things like funny puppets and small blinky lights. Books and games are fun for them to look at, but mostly, they'll want to put them in their mouths.

TODDLERS

Toddlers are more active participants than babies. They like to play alongside other toddlers, but they're not quite sharing or fully interacting in a functional way with other kids yet. They do like to lug around toys and stuffed animals. They also like to show off their newly acquired skills, like kicking. Unfortunately, they don't know how strong they are, so you need to keep an eye on them and put a stop to any potentially dangerous stunts.

Luckily, toddlers are all about imitation, and you're a cool new person in the house, so you're more in control than you think. Keep them busy with role-playing games, like pretend cooking, train conducting, or dress-up. Or spend the afternoon organizing toy cars into categories like big, little, red, and blue. (They can usually recognize patterns, like colors, numbers, or size at this age.) If all else fails, read aloud. Books are very visually stimulating for kids, especially the ones with surprise pop-ups or textile elements. Kids at this age also love pushing sound buttons on books that play funny noises.

PRESCHOOLERS

These are those magical ages between toddler toys and video games when kids love using their imagination. You'll score some points by serving make-believe meals to a group of dolls, helping kids build a fort for their toys, or by initiating a game of hide-and-seek while wearing superhero costumes (suggestion:

raid the towel closet for some homegrown capes!). And they're also into physical activities like riding tricycles, running, and climbing. They probably can't read yet, but they're more engaged in books. So interactive books, like ones that come with stickers, are fair game. Preschoolers are fun because they

TALES FROM THE CRIB

When I first started babysitting (around age fourteen), I went in thinking it was going to be a breeze. I was a teenager, they were little kids; clearly I had authority. But if there's one thing I've learned after years of babysitting, it's to not underestimate the children. For many kids, the parents leaving a babysitter in charge for a night is like when there's a substitute teacher in school. As any high school and even middle school student will tell you, a sub means no assigned seats, no homework, and basically freedom to do whatever you want. Even though they're young, kids feel the same way about a babysitter.

It was only after a few weeks when the kids started asking about watching TV—which was against the family "no TV" rule. Annie, who rarely finished her are so active. But always watch them—you never know when one will try to run into the street, climb up on the counter, or dip their hands in a dangerous cleaning liquid.

Preschoolers may get rigid and say no or throw fits when you try a new tactic. Unless they're hurting someone or being very unfair about sharing or playing nice, just relax and go with it. Don't be afraid to step out of the game and ask what the kid wants.

vegetables when I made dinner, would pull something like, "If I finish these carrots, can I pretty, pretty please watch TV?" I knew, technically, the rule, but I also knew that if Annie finished her vegetables her mom would be very impressed. Once the kids realized I was hesitating before saying no, they'd come in for the kill. "Yeah, please!" Trevor whined. "I finished all of my homework! And Mom and Dad have been letting us watch TV on week nights sometimes." This, I doubted was true. But watching TV was going to make them happy and the things they'd do in order to get me to say yes would make the parents happy, so it was a win-win. These were two young kids who had managed to take full advantage of the lack of parents and convince me to bend the rules. Like I said . . . don't underestimate them.

—Cheyenne, eighteen

While preschoolers like to play with other kids their age, some fighting is usually natural and inevitable. You should orchestrate fun, fair, physical games with very simple rules  (think musical chairs; duck, duck, goose; or pin the tail on the donkey). If toys are involved, it's best to have one for everyone. (Read more about fighting and behavioral challenges on the next page.)

KIDS FIVE AND UP

Older kids are typically comfortable with structured play, like sports, video games, and board games. Sometimes they're a little *too comfy* sitting in front of their iPads. Awesome, educational games like Scrabble and creative activities like birdhouse building or other arts and crafts are ways to prove to them that the world won't end if they drop the game controller. Eventually, kids outgrow playtime, so don't take it personally if they snub you. The older kids get, the more important their friends are. Did you want to hang out with your sitter all day when you were twelve? Lame!

Playtime is supposed to be *fun*. Your ultimate goal shouldn't be to "wow" the kids or be a stickler about game rules. It's an opportunity for you to relax and form a comfortable bond with the children while keeping them safe. Once you've got playtime down, both you and the kids will look forward to your visits, and you'll have a whole list of awesome games and inside jokes to choose from.

10.

Addressing Behavioral Challenges

You're on the after-school shift, and everything is going great. The kid walked briskly home from school. She ate like a champ. And she's in the corner, making a nice little drawing of a cat . . . on the wall.

Quickly, you spring into action, fueled by the fear that your bosses (her parents) will skin you alive. You grab the crayons out of her hand. She flies into a rage. She yells at you. She screams. She cries. She even starts stomping around, throwing things. Everything is officially out of control.

Let's just say, that didn't go well.

Behavioral Basics

It can be maddening and even heartbreaking when a child doesn't listen to you. If a child doesn't want to do their homework, if they're yelling and screaming in the middle of a grocery store, or if they're writing on the walls, it's very easy to feel really stressed and even personally slighted. But getting really mad or beating yourself up over a child's outburst isn't going to help. We used to think that kids needed strict discipline and course correction. But more often, behavioral challenges require patience, listening, constructive feedback and, sometimes, even ignoring a problem until it dies. In the case above, you'd be right to intervene if you catch the kid writing on the wall. She's breaking the rules and damaging the wall! But you should never meet a child's tantrum with another tantrum if you want to defuse it.

To help get through these trying times, here are the basics:

1. **Get the routine down.** Behavioral challenges often happen when there's a rupture in the child's daily routine. Maybe you ate dinner a little later than usual. Maybe the kid didn't get enough sleep. Sometimes certain objects or situations will trigger an emotional reaction. You should get to know the child and stick to the schedule as best as you can.

2. **Let go a little.** Sometimes we react with anger or yelling when things feel out of our control. But we can't always control little kids—not even if you have their routine exactly right. Remember that rigidity, tantrums, and outbursts are pretty natural for kids, and it's not personal. That mindset should help you approach the situation more calmly.

3. **Ask the parents.** The parents are your best resource. They have a method of dealing with behavioral issues, and if possible, you should try to emulate them to be consistent. They should tell you if a child has serious behavioral issues, such as violent outbursts or sensory sensitivities.

4. **Distract.** The "Look over there!" approach isn't foolproof, but it's worth a shot. If you feel a tantrum coming, try distracting the kid with something fun. Do a crazy dance, show them a new toy, or play with their hair.

5. **Stay nearby.** Don't abandon the child in the middle of a difficult emotional moment. Follow them calmly. Let them know that you hear them. But don't go over the top in trying to calm the child down or stopping the event. The moment will eventually pass.

6. **Call the parents.** If you've exhausted all other options, you can call their parents for advice. Only use this tactic as a last resort since they hired you to handle things yourself.

Two (or More) Kids

Babysitting for siblings or playdates is a whole different ball game than an only child. While you can still use one or more constructive tactics (see page 63), getting the job done can  get more complicated as jealousy, bullying, excluding, and fighting occur during playtime or over dinner. Below are some dos and don'ts when dealing with multiple children:

1. **Do encourage friendly play.** If a fight breaks out, you should try to mediate through fair negotiation. If the children are fighting over a toy, for example, you should encourage them to share it or make sure there are enough for everyone. If you play a game with a couple of competitive siblings or playdates, have them work together instead of against each other. For example, you can play a board game and put them on the same team against you.

2. **Don't pick favorites.** Whether you want to or not, you'll probably choose a favorite child who you would rather spend your time with. But you should never, ever show it. Never compare children out loud. Don't give imbalanced consequences. Always make sure you're paying equal attention to both children.

3. **Do keep kids entertained.** A fight can ensue if the children are tired, hungry, or bored. Don't plan strenuous activities around bedtime or before mealtime, and try to keep both kids entertained. If the younger siblings or playdates are annoying the older kids, for example, you should try entertaining the little guys yourself.

4. **Don't tolerate bullying.** Bullying and excluding can be very painful, whether it's between siblings or playdates. It's important to intervene when you see signs of teasing and make sure the children feel protected.

SAFETY FIRST!

Q: *What are the signs of child abuse?*

A: *Child abuse is when a child is verbally berated, beaten, or sexually molested. There is no exact checklist when it comes to looking for signs of abuse. Many times, things like cuts and bruises or even depression are mistaken as signs of abuse when they're not. However, keep an eye on things like constant sustained injuries or inappropriate sexual behavior in the children. If you suspect child abuse, or if a child tells you something happened, talk to your parents or a trusted adult immediately.*

5. **Do separate kids who can't play nice.** If the children are constantly fighting, or if the fighting becomes violent, break them up. It'll distract them from their anger and defuse the situation. Let them know that whoever hits will face consequences, such as not being able to play the game anymore. Live up to your promise, and tell the parents if there is serious violence.

11.
Helping with Homework

After some prodding, you finally got the eight-year-old to do his homework—but he's very obviously not happy about it. He's fiddling with the worksheets, biding time, and hemming and hawing over how hard it is.

Luckily, it's English—your best subject! Immediately, you sit down to help. You correct his mistakes (there are a *lot* of them) and breeze through the work. It's all coming back to you. You're a pronoun, capitalization, apostrophe-making machine! Suddenly, the kid leaves to go to the bathroom. Ten minutes later, you hear the TV blaring. The worst part is, you look at the worksheet and realize in horror that you did the whole thing yourself.

You don't have to be a world-class tutor to be a babysitter. If the parents want a professional teacher to help kids with their homework, they should hire one. However, babysitters should be able to offer children *some* assistance with school assignments and projects. This isn't always easy, since anything is more fun than homework, and it's even harder to do if the child feels challenged by it. Here's how to encourage kids to get the job done, and to make sure the kids learn something:

Stick to the schedule. Ask the parents about the children's homework schedule, and stick to it. You may want to give them a ten-minute warning before homework time to avoid resistance. Remember, kids will be terrible little workers if you force study time when they're tired or hungry, so aim to have homework time after they've eaten and way before bedtime.

Take away distractions. Help a kid out and try to reduce distractions. Keep the siblings away. Turn down the TV, or turn it off completely. Respect the kids' homework space, and keep your distance unless they need you. This will help them concentrate on the task.

Create a fun study environment. Children are more likely to do their homework if their workspace is attractive. Try clearing off a table and putting colorful pencils and school supplies all around. This will provide fun associations with schoolwork. This is really up to the parents to set up, but you can help maintain the space.

Stick around to help. Some homework comes with instructions for parents and caregivers. So find out if you're supposed to get involved. Even if you're not, be generally available for questions while giving them space. If you're babysitting for young children, look over their homework when they're done. If you're dealing with older kids, be honest if something is too hard for you. A lot of grown-ups don't remember how to do long division, so don't beat yourself up if you don't know the answer. Instead, help them find someone who does, or look for instructional videos online.

Don't answer for them. Even if a child is struggling with their homework, you shouldn't answer the questions for them or they'll never learn to do it themselves. Guide the child to the right answer, and wait patiently. Once they get it right, make sure they understand how they got there. You want to make sure they're learning and not just filling in the blanks!

12.

Bathing Children Safely

You've been playing in the mud with a three-year-old, and while it was probably the best time you've ever had in a dirt pile, Karlee needs a bath.

But when you start to fill the tub, you discover that the girl who was so unafraid to play with giant bugs a few minutes ago is petrified of the bath drain. She's convinced that it will suck her into a terrifying netherworld filled with child-eating drain monsters. So when you suggest a bath, she throws a tantrum and sullies up the couch with her muddy pants. She couldn't care less about the stains because, to her, you're a mean, mean babysitter.

Kids can get pretty dirty, and they may need your help getting clean—whether they want it or not. Some parents want their babysitter to take care of the bathing ritual. Others prefer to take care of it themselves. (You can always use a warm washcloth as an alternative to a bath.) If your bosses haven't specified what they want you to do, ask them. You may even need a demo. Also, you may have some outstanding questions—such as whether the siblings should bathe together or separately. This could lead to more questions, like who's going to watch the kid  who's not in the tub? Don't leave any stone unturned.

Bath time can be scary for kids, so you need a plan to keep things fun and disaster-free—and safe from drain beasts (and if you can't clean up the couch stains, be honest to the parents about what happened. They'll understand.)

Here are some tips:

For babies, get some experience. Typically, a parent shouldn't ask an inexperienced babysitter to bathe a newborn or a baby who can't sit up. Babies usually lie upright in special tubs, where the caregiver gives them a sponge bath. Don't do this until you have plenty of hands-on experience.

Keep water levels low. Little kids can easily drown in a tub, so never fill it all the way. The water should only be 2 to 3 inches (5 to 7.6 cm) high for babies, and for older children, the water should come to their waists when they sit down.

Test the temperature. Before putting a kid in the tub, make sure the temperature is comfortably warm. You don't want to burn or freeze them to tears! Test the temperature of the water by wetting the palm side of your wrist or use your elbow. These spots are more sensitive than your fingers.

Don't push, just help. Tubs are slippery, especially for active little kids. Hold their hands as they climb in and out of the tub, or lift them in and out. And don't let go until they're sitting in a stable position. If a child is nervous about getting in the tub, don't force them in. Be gentle, and don't criticize their fears, even if drain monsters are the funniest things you've ever heard of.

Make it fun. If a kid is reluctant to get in the tub, offer to bring some waterproof, safe toys into the tub. Or promise to read their favorite book or sing their favorite song while they take a bath. Whatever it takes. Even after they get clean, you should let them play in the tub for a little while. It'll make bath time something to look forward to.

Wash their hair (optional). Children don't need their hair washed every day, so ask the parents about this before-

hand. If the answer is yes, you mainly want to avoid getting water or shampoo in kids' eyes—and make sure you're using the child-friendly shampoo, not their dad's. Tilt their heads back, and use a plastic cup or bowl to pour water on their hair. Guard their eyes by placing your other hand or a washcloth lightly on their forehead. Lather the specified shampoo in their hair, and rinse it off (again, use the cup and keep their heads tilted back). Dry off their foreheads and hairlines.

Supervise, supervise, supervise! You've gotten them in the tub, you've washed their hair, and you've read them three books. You're a bath-time gold medalist! But your job isn't done. Stay in the room to make sure the kids sit relatively still. Also, make sure they don't bonk their heads on the faucet, and most important, make sure they keep their heads above the water. Even leaving the room for a minute to answer the phone or the doorbell can lead to a potential drowning. If you absolutely have to leave the room, wrap up the child in a towel and bring them with you.

Prep for the post-tub procedure. Before you gently coax the kids out of the bath, have a clean towel handy, as well as their next outfits. When they're out of the tub, dry their bodies and hair gently with the towel. Some parents will ask you to use rash cream or moisturizer for dry skin. Afterward, dress the kids (see page 53 for tips) and maybe help them brush their teeth if it's bedtime. If the children have long, tangly hair, run a comb through it while it's still wet. You can spray or rub leave-in conditioner into their hair before you start brushing to help minimize shrieking.

Bathe in case of emergency. Sometimes a bath wasn't part of the parents' instructions, but the kid really needs one. If that happens on your watch, call the parents to explain the situation. And ask them if they have any specific instructions. Below are some examples of bathing emergencies:

- The children have urinated or soiled themselves, and they're not wearing diapers (or the diapers didn't do the job).
- The children are extremely filthy or sticky. This may happen if they have been playing outside.
- You suspect lice, scabies, fleas, or another infestation that could put their health (and yours) at risk. In this case, the parents should come home.

SAFETY FIRST!

Q. What do I do if a kid begins to drown?

A. Become CPR certified before accepting a babysitting job. Hopefully, you'll never have to use it, but it is important to be prepared in case of emergency situations like this. If a child is drowning, remove them from the water. Ask if they're all right, and try to rouse them. If they're unconscious, not breathing, or without

a pulse and if someone is there to help, ask them to call 911 while you begin CPR. If you're alone or if you're not already trained in CPR, do this:

1. Place the child on their back on a hard surface.
2. For children ages one through eight, place the heel of your hand on the child's chest, right between the child's nipples. For a younger child, place just two of your fingers in the same spot
3. Push down, using your body weight. You want to push down at least 2 inches (5 cm) each time for children ages one through eight, and for babies, you'll want to

push 1.5 inches (3.8 cm). Push one hundred times per minute, which is the same speed as the beat of "All Star" by Smash Mouth or "Crazy in Love" by Beyoncé.*

If you are ever in doubt about what to do or how to do it, ask the 911 dispatcher.

---

*Instructions taken from the 2020 American Heart Association Guidelines for Cardiopulmonary Resuscitation and Emergency Cardiovascular Care. part 4, section 5.2.

13.
Putting Kids to Bed

It's your favorite time of day: the kid's bedtime. Soon you'll have a few hours of precious peace before the parents come home. You'll be able to text back the friend who's been trying to reach you. You'll finally check the score of the big game.

But Diego is not looking forward to bedtime as much as you are. Sensing that it's time for bed, he just came up with a laundry list of activities to do. He broke out the video games, the board games, even the homework that he was so unwilling to do a few minutes ago. He's clearly wound up and exhausted, but when you say it's time for bed, he screams no and starts to cry. You're so tired yourself that you don't want to put up a fight. You reason, *Maybe if I indulge him and play with him some more, he'll tire himself out!*

But before you know it, two hours have gone by. The parents are pulling up in the driveway, and the kid, now delirious from lack of sleep, is trying to parachute down the stairs with a garbage bag. Enjoy explaining your way out of this one.

Kids can be very determined about not getting their z's. While it's almost impossible to get children totally psyched for bedtime, you can make it a lot smoother.

Learn the routine. Children will go down easier if bedtime happens according to their regular schedule. As always, your biggest source of information is the parents. Some questions to ask parents include these:

- What time does the child go to bed?
- Do they need a nap? If so, how often and how long do they sleep?
- What's their usual bedtime ritual? Do they brush their teeth by themselves? Do they wear special pajamas? Do they need a story, lullaby, night-light, or all of these?
- Do they need you to stay with them until they fall asleep, or are they OK alone?
- Do they have nightmares? If so, what's the best way to put them back to sleep?
- Are they night trained?

Be patient. Remember that even grown-ups have trouble putting their own kids to bed. It may take five minutes, or it may take a couple of hours—which is tough when you want to watch the game. Remain patient and calm, and stick to the routine as much as you can. Don't yell. As long as you tried as hard as you could, the parents should understand if you had trouble getting the child to sleep on time. (If they don't, they might be unreasonable!)

Keep it quiet. If you want to encourage sleep, don't blast the TV or chat loudly on the phone. The noise will not only wake up the children, but they'll also want to climb out of bed because they want to watch TV too! Also, if you're babysitting small children, keeping noise levels down allows you to hear them cry.

Breaching routine is OK if necessary. If you stuck to the routine for over an hour and the kid still won't go to sleep, there's a decent chance that the kid is changing things up because their parents aren't home. If the routine isn't working, maybe loosen the grip a bit. Perhaps the kid can snuggle on the couch quietly with you just this once. The parents will understand that you tried.

Give parents an update. Let parents know if you notice any sleep issues. Maybe the toddler seemed fussy and was constantly rubbing their eyes long before their scheduled nap time. Or maybe they loved your singing voice. The parents may decide to change the routine based on what you tell them.

SAFETY FIRST!

Q. Is it true that babies can die from sleeping?

A. As shocking as it may sound, even sleeping can be dangerous for babies. Sudden infant death syndrome (SIDS) is when a baby under the age of one dies suddenly while sleeping and the cause of death can't be determined. The reason you should care is that about one in five SIDS cases happen while an infant is being cared for by someone other than a parent. No one knows what causes SIDS, but there are ways to promote a safe sleep. For instance, babies who sleep on their stomachs are more likely to die of SIDS. So, when putting infants to sleep, make sure to do the following:

- Place them on their backs. Even if they're on their sides, they may roll onto their stomachs and risk SIDS.
- Remove surrounding toys, clothes, rags, or anything that could block a baby's airway.
- Choose sleepwear with covered feet or special sleep bags instead of blankets, which can easily block an airway. Babies aren't supposed to use blankets in their cribs until the age of one.

14.

Keeping Kids Healthy

You're babysitting for a four-year-old socialite. You've never seen anyone with so many freaking playdates. One day you have to take her to the zoo with her best friend. The next, it's a pool party. The next, it's a giant sleepover. She's got so many engagements that she deserves her own reality show.

Unfortunately, this is the same girl who doesn't want to wear a mask. She also hates medicine, hand soap, rest, and vitamin C. One day, she comes home from a playdate with a not-so-surprising stomach bug. Fever, vomiting, diarrhea—she's got it all.

When it comes to kids, accidents happen. So does mucus, vomit, germs, and diarrhea. They also often get cuts and scrapes. They may have asthma, colic, or allergies. And all of these things can flare up on your watch. When they do, it's important to know how to handle it. While you should call 911 when major disasters strike, like broken bones or anything that involves a lot of blood, it helps to know how to deal with minor emergencies. Here are some common medical problems that babysitters face while on the job, along with tips on how to solve them:

Allergies

Some children get bad reactions from things like shellfish, soy, nuts, dust, pet dander, and pollen. Symptoms can range from itchiness and rashes to vomiting and life-threatening shock.

WHAT TO DO

- Take preventative measures. Become CPR certified before taking a babysitting job. Avoid potential allergic reactions by asking parents what the triggers are and keeping the kids away from anything that could set off an attack.

- Get the 411 on any medication. Parents may ask you to give the child over-the-counter or prescription allergy medicine. Kids with more serious allergies may even need regular shots, which should not be administered by an inexperienced babysitter.

- If there is a risk of a child going into anaphylactic shock their parents should outline the emergency protocol. Often, this involves administering an epinephrine shot to the middle of the outer thigh with an EpiPen. The injector is easy to use and has clear instructions on the side. Any delay in administering epinephrine can be life threatening, so you should use the EpiPen before calling 911.

If a child is light-headed, nauseated, short of breath, breaking out in a rash, vomiting, or unconscious, they may be going into anaphylactic shock. This can eventually cause a child to stop breathing and may even stop their heartbeat. In this case, you should call 911 after administering an epinephrine shot (if needed) but before starting CPR.

Asthma

Asthma is a disease that causes inflammation of the airways. Parents will usually let you know if their child is asthmatic. If they are, make sure you get specific instructions about how to handle it. During an attack, a child's respiratory system swells up and blocks air from flowing freely. An asthma attack can be pretty scary. The child may cough or wheeze excessively, and in serious cases, they may not be able to breathe. An asthma attack can be triggered by exercise, irritating fumes, or from allergies, so stay away from anything that can set one off.

WHAT TO DO

- Ask parents for a complete rundown of asthma meds as well as the details of their emergency action plan.
- Set reminders for yourself if you need to juggle a number of medications.

- Carry the child's inhaler—a pocket-sized device that squirts asthma medicine into the child's mouth—on you at all times. Some kids may need to use fast-acting inhalers when they're about to exercise or when they feel an attack coming on.
- Have the child's parents show you how to use any additional asthma equipment that may be needed. Children around toddler age and younger can't use inhalers because the dosage is too unpredictable. You may have to apply a face mask that attaches to a machine called a nebulizer. It sounds scary, but it's a simple device.

WHEN TO WORRY

- If a child is having difficulty breathing, even if they have not been diagnosed with asthma, call 911 immediately.
- If, despite treatment (for instance the child has used their inhaler), the child with asthma is still having a severe reaction—which can include widening nostrils, straining their abdominal muscles, and stopping in the middle of a sentence to catch their breath—always call 911, even if you are unsure if the attack is serious. Better safe than sorry.

Colic

When an otherwise healthy, well-fed baby cries nonstop for no reason, the baby may have colic. Colic is one of the great (and, for parents and babysitters, frustrating) mysteries of medicine. Nobody really knows what causes it, and the only

known symptoms are a healthy baby who cries for more than three hours a day, three days a week or more, for more than three weeks. The baby's crying jags generally happen around the same time every day and can be accompanied by screaming and fist clenching. There is no cure, but it usually goes away on its own when the child is about three months old.

WHAT TO DO

- Try all the things you'd normally try for any crying baby, like giving them a pacifier, rocking, feeding, singing, or even leaving them alone in their crib for a minute.
- Exercise your kindest patience, and try to not get over-whelmed. Colicky babies will often keep crying, so you'll need to keep calm and not get too frustrated.

WHEN TO WORRY

- If a baby cries longer than three hours, call the parents to see if they have any solutions. A colicky baby can make it sound as though the sky is falling, but the condition is not dangerous. Episodes usually last up to three hours.
- If you suspect that they're injured or ill, call the parents, any emergency contacts, and 911. Also, let the parents know if the baby is refusing to eat or sleep due to inces-sant crying.

Cuts and Scrapes

Since the dawn of time, children have been getting cuts and scrapes while playing sports, falling downstairs, or even just walking around the house. These are slight skin injuries, and they sometimes result in bleeding.

WHAT TO DO

- Wash your hands before you start treating the wound.
- Hold a clean bandage or cloth on a bloody wound for about ten to twenty minutes or until the blood stops flowing.
- Clean it with a damp sterile cotton pad or antiseptic wipe. (Make sure to get all the nasty dirt out so the cut doesn't get infected.)
- Apply a triple antibiotic cream, like Neosporin, to kill any remaining bacteria in the wound and to keep bad bacteria away.
- Cover the wound with a bandage—preferably colorful, if the parents have some! (Kitties and dinosaurs are safe bets.)

WHEN TO WORRY

- If the cut doesn't stop bleeding or if a considerable amount of dirt or junk stays lodged in the wound, you should call 911 and follow their instructions.
- If the wound is bigger or deeper than a minor scrape, you may

need to call 911 so the child can get stitches. Instead, some parents may want you to call a trusted neighbor who might be able to help.

- If the child has trouble moving the wounded limb, you should call 911, the parents, or the emergency contact. They may have sprained or fractured something.
- If the child cuts themselves on rusty metal, they may have to get a tetanus shot—or if they're bitten by an animal that may have rabies, they may need treatment. If this happens on your watch, call 911 or the emergency contacts.

SAFETY FIRST!

Q: *What do I do if a child ingests toxic materials?*

A: *Unfortunately, it happens all the time. Children mistake cough medicine for juice or housecleaning products for toothpaste. These mistakes can lead to serious illness or even death. If you see a child ingest a toxic chemical, call 911 and also 800-222-1222, which will link you to your nearest Poison Control Center in the US. Be ready to tell them the child's age, how long ago they ingested the poison, and what kind of toxic material it is. Meanwhile, make sure that you always read the label and that all poisonous materials are out of the child's reach.*

Call the parents or seek medical help if any of the symptoms mentioned are present.

Diarrhea

You probably already know what diarrhea is—runny or watery bowel movements—and if the child you're babysitting is complaining of stomach pains and constantly going to the bathroom, they might have it. It can be caused by anything from food poisoning to a stomach virus. A bad case of the runs can lead to dehydration, especially in babies.

WHAT TO DO

- Avoid diarrhea by washing your hands (and the child's hands) often, especially before touching food and after using the bathroom, coughing, sneezing, or handling pets.
- Wash food thoroughly before serving it, and don't serve anything that could potentially lead to an upset stomach. For example, if a child is lactose intolerant, don't serve them dairy.
- Store and heat food to proper temperatures. Bacteria can grow on foods in the temperature "danger zone" between 41 and 135°F (5–57.2°C). Make sure that perishable foods—such as meat or dairy—are kept in the fridge when not in use. And be sure to get that leftover pizza in the fridge in a timely fashion too. Anything left out for more than two hours should go in the trash.

- Call the child's parents for advice on administering any diarrhea medication. They might have home remedies they'd like you to try first—but sometimes all a child needs is time.
- Consult the parents about the fluids you should give a child with diarrhea. Continue to give breast milk or formula to babies to keep them hydrated. For older children, see if there are any oral rehydration drinks such as Pedialyte in the house to help replace lost nutrients. If not, keep the water flowing. Often soda, sports drinks, and fruit juices can make diarrhea worse because they don't have the right sugars and salts to help rehydrate a child.

WHEN TO WORRY

- The child is vomiting.
- They refuse to drink liquids.
- They have a fever above 102°F (39°C).
- Their stomachaches are extremely painful, or blood or mucus is in their diarrhea (yes, you have to look at it).
- The diarrhea doesn't go away after a couple of days.

Call the parents or seek medical help if they have any of these symptoms.

Fever

If a child's temperature is running higher than normal, they may have a fever. Normal body temperatures can range between 97°F and 99°F (36°C and 37°C). It may be a fever if a child has

- a rectal, ear, or temporal artery (an artery on each side of the forehead) temperature of 100.4°F (38°C) or higher,
- an oral temperature of 100°F (37.8°C) or higher, or
- an armpit temperature of 99°F (37.2°C) or higher.

Usually, this means that their body is heating up from fighting off an infection. Fevers in teens and adults aren't typically dangerous, but for young children and babies, a fever can indicate a serious infection. Sometimes a fever even indicates a major illness like pneumonia or meningitis when coupled with additional symptoms.

WHAT TO DO

- If the child's forehead is warm to the touch and they complain about not feeling well, take their temperature. If it's high, let the parents know about the abnormal temperature change. Low-grade fevers will often go away on their own without treatment, but it's still important to let parents know.
- Administer a fever-reducing medicine like children's acetaminophen or children's ibuprofen if the parents ask you to. Follow all the dosage instructions on the bottle.
- Make sure the child has plenty of water, other hydrating liquids like Pedialyte, or both.

- The child is younger than three months and has a temperature higher than 100.4°F (38°C).
- The child is older than three months and they have a temperature up to 102°F (38.9°C) and seems uncomfortable or overly fatigued, or if they have a temperature over 102°F and it doesn't drop after a day.
- The child is vomiting and refusing to eat or drink.
- The child has a fever after being left in a hot car or if the fever is accompanied by seizures, call 911 immediately.

Call the parents or seek medical help if they have any of these symptoms.

Nosebleeds

A nosebleed is usually when blood gushes out of somebody's septum, the chamber that separates the nostrils. Kids can get nosebleeds for many reasons. They might trip and fall on their face, pick their nose, shove a LEGO up their nostril, or simply be in a dry environment. They're messy, but they're rarely dangerous.

WHAT TO DO

- Sit the child upright, and have them lean forward.
- Pinch the child's nose, or have the child pinch their own nose shut to put pressure on the bleeding point and help stop the blood flow.
- Have them breathe through their mouth for about ten

minutes—which might be impossible with some kids, but do your best.

- If the bleeding hasn't stopped by then, have the child (lightly) blow their nose, pinch it, and repeat. Don't let the kid pick their nose again no matter how badly they want to.

WHEN TO WORRY

- The child's nose bleeds for more than thirty minutes.
- You think their nose is broken, or if they have persistent nosebleeds throughout the day.

Call the parents or seek medical help if they have any of these symptoms.

15.
Avoiding Preventable Emergencies

Accidents happen. Kids fall down. People get sick. Things break. However, within reason, you should take certain precautions to avoid accidents. It'll be worth it in the end.

Watch kids closely. You'll be amazed at how easily little kids can destroy things. This is one reason why you should pay attention to them at all times. Save personal phone calls and texts for when the kids are fast asleep. And even if your favorite show is on, don't leave kids to play alone. You should never assume that they're totally safe from injury.

Don't come to work sick. Children are particularly susceptible to germs that cause illnesses, like colds or flus. If the kids get sick, they could easily spread their germs to their siblings or classmates. If you're feeling ill, take time off.

Ask for help. Nobody knows how to deal with every problem. If you don't know how to handle a safety issue, don't guess. If Johnny gets an injury and you're not sure whether to wrap it in bandages or pump him full of fluids, you should call his parents, trusted adults, or medical professionals. You might even consult your own parents.

Say no to dangerous situations. This may seem obvious, but there's no other way to put it. At some point, children will want to play with the stove, run with scissors, run across the street at a red light or light something on fire. They might even try to convince you that their parents let them do it all the time. Always trust your gut instinct, and say no if something seems dangerous. Let them know that it might be something they can do when their parents are around, but not when you are. If it's already too late and damage has been done, tell the parents what happened (even if you may not have used your best judgment—remember

that everyone makes mistakes). Parents need to know what their kids have been up to, especially if they've been injured.

Don't panic. Even if you're very stressed in an emergency, try to remain in control. You're still the authority figure, and you don't want to scare the kids any further. Panicking will also impede your ability to make good decisions. Breathe, and call someone who can help.

TALES FROM THE CRIB

When preparing for movie time, I lit a Jiffy Pop—popcorn you make on the stove—on fire. Not the popcorn, but the tinfoil on top. I prepared it exactly as the directions instructed. I don't know how it happened. But, it did, so I waited for the smoke alarms to go off. Nothing. Taking extra precautions, I opened the back door and cleared the smoke out of the house . . . or so I thought. Ten minutes later, every smoke alarm in the entire house was blaring. Just taking out the battery wasn't enough. Unplugging the whole thing didn't work. Oh, no. I had to dismantle the whole smoke alarm, unplug it, and open every window on all three floors! And while I was running frantically around the house dismantling smoke alarms and opening windows and doors, the two boys I was sitting silently watched me. After I told the mother, I left with her fake concerned laugh ringing in my ears.

—Megan, fourteen

Emergency Call Sheet

Sure, everyone says not to panic during an emergency. But it's hard not to freak out if something really bad is going down. This is why you should have phone numbers for the parents, the police, the fire department, a neighbor, and an extra emergency contact in an easy-to-find place so you're not frantically searching for the numbers later on. You can copy the sheet below and fill in important numbers for all your clients, or enter these numbers into your cell phone for each client.

Who to Call in Case of an Emergency

Police _____

Fire Department _____

Parent(s) or Guardian(s) _____

_____

Neighbor _____

Pediatrician _____

Poison Control Center _____

TALES FROM THE CRIB

This situation is what every babysitter dreads—when the first news that you have to deliver to the parents is that their child has a huge lump on her head . . . and it's your fault. A few evenings ago I was babysitting two little girls, Sasha and Ava. Ava is five and Sasha is seven. After a dinner of bean-and-cheese burritos at our favorite local taqueria, the girls suggested we play with their new softball batting machine. I agreed, and went first to get a feel for the contraption. I took a few practice swings, and on the third swing I finally hit the end of the rod—and something else . . . Sasha's head! She immediately fell to the ground and let out a screaming cry. I ran to her and saw the lump on her head beginning to form already! I apologized over and over again, and Ava happily pretended to be the big sister for the night, running to get Sasha's favorite stuffed animal friends. I carried Sasha into the house, got an ice pack, and put her on the couch. Sasha was a great sport about the whole thing—when she heard she had to put ice on it, she decided that she would have an ice pack on her head literally the entire rest of the night. Even after I put her to bed she would come out when her ice got warm and get a new pack. When her parents got home and I had to break the news, they weren't too upset. They said it would teach her to not stand so close to the batting machine. I claimed responsibility, but they still didn't blame me. Surprisingly, I think how I handled the situation and how I continued to ask how Sasha was doing helped my reputation as a babysitter. Moral of the story: Don't hit a kid in the head with a bat, but if you do, you can still score babysitting points by handling the situation calmly and responsibly!

— Althea, sixteen

16.

Taking Care of Yourself

You've officially had it. Harper won't go to bed, Cameron's nose won't stop bleeding, and Sean won't stop crying. You're so frustrated that you can hardly breathe. You feel a panic attack coming on. You feel faint. You feel hoarse. You're sure you feel a cold coming on. You resolve never to babysit for the rest of your life . . . starting immediately.

In protest, you sit on the couch and do nothing for hours. It feels great. But when you've finally calmed down, you realize that everything had gotten so much worse in your absence. The kids are still awake, wound up, eating sugary foods, and fighting furiously. Harper cut her leg tripping on the floor, and she's covered in blood. So, did checking out and ignoring the kids really help your health and stress levels? Probably not.

Babysitters are susceptible to germs and tantrums too! And you also have to manage hazardous materials such as snot, vomit, and blood. Here are some ways to keep yourself safe around kids:

Speak Up about Your Health

If you have chronic issues, like asthma, an immune system issue, or allergies, you should tell the parents before you babysit. If you are sick with something temporary like a cold, they may not want you to sit. But maybe they can accommodate certain issues by vacuuming up that dog hair before you come over, or maybe they'll have you skip the usual trip to the park so you can rest a little more. If they don't know what you're going through, how can they help you?

Take Necessary Precautions

Wash your hands frequently with soap and water or with alcohol-based hand sanitizer, especially after you've handled saliva, diapers, dirty dishes, or anything germy. If you want to be extra safe, you can wear rubber gloves when you're handling bodily fluids and when treating cuts and scrapes. Get tested frequently for COVID-19. Wear masks indoors whenever possible. Also, stay healthy to keep that immune system strong. Eat a healthy diet, drink plenty of water, and exercise!

Prevent Sickness from Spreading

Curing an illness in its early stages is one surefire way to prevent it from spreading to you. If you notice that a child appears sick (coughing, vomiting, diarrhea, congestion, or scratching are telltale signs!), tell the parents immediately. They may suggest an over-the-counter medication or other cure. Ask about the family's COVID-19 vaccination statuses. You may want them or the kids to get tested before you sit.

Managing Stress

Not even Mary Poppins can deny that childcare is hard work. The stress can take a mental toll on the most hardcore, experienced babysitters, but you need to stay in control if you want to keep the kids safe. It's natural to feel fatigued, annoyed, or downright angry with the children or the parents. But you can maintain your sanity while being a fun, safe sitter. If you are feeling particularly overwhelmed, slow down, breathe, and count to ten. Keep in mind the following tips and tricks. They will help you to be prepared for whatever comes at you.

1. **Love your body.** While skipping a meal or staying up late before a babysitting job may not seem like a big deal, it could lead to dangers down the road. For example, sleep deprivation, low blood sugar levels, and dehydration can all make you feel dizzy, tired, or faint. This affects your ability to perform on the job, clouds your judgment, and increases the likelihood of something bad going down. At the very least, you won't enjoy the job as much.

2. **Breathe deeply (and often).** Some situations can be so bad that you'll want to check out, walk out, and let the kids take care of themselves! Although it sounds cliché, taking a deep breath is a great way to calm your nerves before you reach your breaking point. Anytime you're feeling particularly anxious, stop what you're doing and inhale

deeply through your nose. The full inhale should last for about seven seconds. Then hold your breath for two seconds and let all the air out in a big sigh. Keep repeating this breathing exercise until you feel your anger subside.

3. **Give yourself a break.** Just as some parents hire you so they can get time away from the kids, you need a break from your childcare duties too. Make sure to leave plenty of space for your social life and interests, even if that means just blocking off an afternoon to veg in front of the TV. Regularly scheduled downtime allows you to come back to the job totally refreshed and ready to take on any babysitting challenge.

4. **Seek professional help.** If you're feeling perpetually stressed, frustrated, or depressed, it may help to get counseling. Your school or a certified private counselor can help you sort out some tough feelings about your job or life. Don't let your frustrations fester. If you don't talk about on-the-job stresses with someone you trust, you may build up serious resentment toward the children, the parents, and babysitting. If you have no interest in the job, how can you protect the children, let alone have fun while you're at it?

5. **Know when to quit.** If the job is really making you crazy and none of the above stress tactics work, it may be time to quit. Try to end the work relationship on a friendly note, if possible—but sometimes, families make it hard to do that. (See page 129 for advice on how to walk away.)

Business
Basics

17.

Landing a Job

You're a natural charmer. People seem to fall in love with you immediately. You're nice to all the kids in the neighborhood. You're polite to the adults. You're well known for your community involvement. So, why hasn't anyone asked you to babysit their kids? Is it your breath? Chances are, no. The truth is, babysitting jobs don't always fall in your lap, no matter how sweet you are. You have to be proactive. A lot of other people are hunting for babysitting jobs too, so you have to appear professional and sell your skills so you stand out. Here are seven steps to help you find that perfect babysitting gig and seal the deal:

Step 1. Talk to Your Parents or Caregivers about Your Plans

If you're a teenager, you probably don't want to tell your parents everything about your life. But until you're an adult, you should loop them into your plans to launch a babysitting business. They can help you get started, polish your presentation, garner contacts, and make sure that you're safe. Plus, a good employer will probably want to talk to your parents if you're under eighteen.

Step 2. Create a Special Email Address

Before you start putting yourself out there, create a separate email account that can be used strictly for babysitting. This way, emails from potential clients and employers won't get lost in your crowded inbox, and it's less likely that you'll make a silly mistake, like sending a stupid video of yourself to a child's parents when you intended to send it to a friend. Also, if your current email address happens to be something like Cutie555 or ILoveRobotz, employers won't take you seriously. Your professional email address shouldn't raise any eyebrows. You can use something that is babysitting-related such as NYCsitter@gmail.com, but if you can't think of anything clever, using your name is a safe bet.

Step 3. Prepare Your Résumé

A résumé is a simple way to highlight your babysitting background and skill sets, making it easy for a potential employer to see why you're perfect for the job. It should include your contact information, a one-line objective that sums up who you are and what kind of job you're looking for, past babysitting experience, and any additional skills that are relevant to child-care—think CPR certification, language fluency, or experience with children with disabilities. You can also list your job as a coffeehouse barista or weed puller (it shows responsibility), but make sure it includes plenty of childcare. Your experience should be listed in chronological order starting with the most recent gig, and it should include some details, like the ages of the children and the hours that you babysat. Don't worry if you don't have too many things to list. The entire point of a résumé is to keep things brief (ideally one page). And remember, caring for siblings or cousins counts as experience! Check out the sample résumé on the next page, and then try creating one on your own.

Step 4. Choose Your References

Some employers may ask you for references. This probably means that they're interested in hiring you, but they want to talk to people you've worked for to make sure you're as great as you seem. Pick two or more contacts who you know will gush about you. Ideally, they should be able to talk about your childcare experience, your painstaking professionalism, and your glowing personality. (Don't pick the parent who complains about everything, including you.) If you don't have employment references, think of the other adults in your life—your teachers, your neighbors, or your coaches, for example. They can vouch for things like your promptness, your sense of humor, and your excellent character.

Sophia Sitter
6 Caregiver Road
Kidland, NY 10000

OBJECTIVE:
Certified babysitter and entertainer looking for part-time work in the Kidland area.

EXPERIENCE:
March–June 2022: Part-Time Babysitter in Kidland, NY

Babysat for a three-year-old and an infant after school until bedtime three nights a week

July–November 2021: Part-Time Babysitter in Playville, NY

Babysat for an eight-year-old diabetic child on weekends for four hours a day

June–August 2021: Part-Time Children's Entertainer in Kidland, NY

Guitarist-singer for children's birthday parties for Parties 'n' Things Company

EDUCATION:
Student at Kidland High School, Class of 2025

On the honor roll, on the basketball team, in the theater department, and in the Key Club

CPR Certification from American Red Cross, May 2020

Earned my Infant/Child and Adult CPR Certification

ADDITIONAL SKILLS:
Speak Greek fluently, guitarist-singer, basketball player, and actor

The new employer will probably want the phone numbers or email addresses of your references, so give your references a heads up before you hand over their information. You want to find out if these people even want to vouch for you, and it's common courtesy to let them know ahead of time that someone might be contacting them so they can be prepared.

Step 5. Talk to People You Know

The fastest way to get a babysitting job (or any job) is through people you know and trust. If you tell your friends and family that you're looking for a job, you may get one quicker than you expect. Make a list of people you know who have kids. You probably know more of them than you think! Consider your family; your friends' parents; your parents' friends; the people who attend your church, mosque, or synagogue; and the parents at all your sports events or band concerts. Gather their contact information into one document, and spend a half hour each night calling them and sending emails—not a lot, just once, with a follow-up a week or so later. Tell them politely that you're looking for a babysitting job. If they don't need your services, maybe they know somebody who does. If you already have some babysitting experience and are planning to make it a regular gig, you may also want to create business cards, a website, or a social media brand and advertise your services.

Step 6. Jobs on the Internet?

Many babysitting jobs are posted online. However, most websites like Care.com require you to be over eighteen to post your profile as a babysitter. There are community-based options like NextDoor.com where people are seeking local sitter help. A local parent might post a general request to the neighborhood, and your parent or guardian can respond on your behalf. Or your parent might post that they have a teenager who is interested in babysitting locally. But jobs online should *always* be navigated with a parent or guardian—any responsible employer will not communicate directly with a teenage babysitter but will ask to speak with and possibly meet your parents. If they try to communicate directly with a teenager, that's a red flag that they're irresponsible at best and, at worst, dangerous.

Step 7. Nail That Big Interview

So you've made it to an interview. The parents are already impressed with you on paper, and they want to get a sense of who you are in real life. During an interview, your personality can matter just as much as your qualifications. Parents want to see that you're mature, friendly, and on top of things. More important, they want to make sure you're a good match for their family. You want to bring your A game and let your great personality shine through. Here are some tips for nailing an interview:

1. **Dress to impress.** You don't need to put on a suit when meeting parents for the first time, but you shouldn't look

sloppy either. Instead, dress as you would on the job: comfortably (no high heels), modestly (no teeny shorts or low-cut shirts), and put-together (no pajama pants or ripped shirts). You want your outfit to go relatively  unnoticed so the parents can focus entirely on your personality. Be groomed and bathed.

2. **Arrive prepared.** Show up five to ten minutes before the scheduled interview. You don't want to keep the parents waiting. Plus, arriving first gives you some quiet time to collect your thoughts, especially if you had to brave traffic (or a similarly chaotic situation) to get to the meeting. Chances are, if you've made it this far, the parents have already seen your résumé. But it doesn't hurt to have one ready in a neat folder, and don't forget to list your references! You may also want to bring a notebook and pen so you can write down any extra details. This will make you look organized and serious about the job.

3. **Be interested and interesting.** There's a misconception that interviews are all about talking. Actually, a good portion of an interview is sitting back and listening. Some employers are chatty during interviews. They want to talk about their kids, their jobs, their spouses, and some of them just want to gossip. Ultimately, the parents want to get along with you, so try to listen. Of course, that doesn't mean you shouldn't talk. The parents probably want to hear about you too. Be yourself.

SAFETY FIRST!

Q. *What if I'm worried about my safety?*

A. *The parents may seem perfectly nice through emails and phone calls, but they're still strangers. Have a trusted adult accompany you, as long as they know that this is your interview. If you have a funny feeling about anything, don't be afraid to bail. Plenty of other jobs are out there. Your personal safety should come first.*

4. **Not sure what to say?** The following talking points can help:
   - Talk about one challenge you faced in a former job and how you fixed it.
   - Tell one funny (but ultimately positive) story about babysitting.
   - Share two (or more) fun facts about yourself, such as your musical skills or your Boy or Girl Scout merits.
   - Ask at least three questions about the children that the parents didn't address in the job ad.
   - Ask at least one question about the parents' jobs.
5. **Tell the truth**. Be honest about your schedule and qualifications during an interview. For example, don't say

you can work Fridays if you know you can't. Or don't say you're certified in CPR when you're not. You could wind up frustrating employers, or worse, seriously endangering a child.

6. **Be open-minded.** Families come in all shapes and sizes. Maybe you are more conservative than they are. Maybe they observe diets that you don't. Maybe they have jobs that you don't morally agree with. If you want to babysit for a family, you must be open-minded during the interview. If it's just not possible, tell them nicely that you have different beliefs and that perhaps you're not the best person for the job.

7. **Make a polite exit.** The interview is over when the parents say it's over. Parents may want to think it through before giving you a final decision on the job. Even if you're dying of anticipation, don't push them for an answer. Simply say it was a pleasure to meet them.

18.
Deciding How Much to Charge

Figuring out how much money to ask for is one of the toughest parts of any job. It's particularly hard for babysitters because there are few set rules and laws to back you up. While some parents will say up front how much they're willing to pay, which would leave it up to you to accept the rate (or not), it's still wise to have a price in mind. Here are several factors to consider when picking your pay:

1. **The going rate.** On average, part-time sitters earn $17. However, that amount varies depending on where you live and how many kids you're watching, so you'll want to do some research to find out how much your competitors are charging, especially those sitters with the same level of experience as you have. You'll want to stay within this range so your rate doesn't seem totally out there. Care.com and Sittercity.com have average babysitter rate

calculators. Expect to make a little less on your very first gig.

2. **Minimum wage.** In some countries (including the US) minimum wage is the lowest salary that employers can pay their employees. If they pay less, they're breaking the law. Minimum wage doesn't apply to part-time baby-sitters in the US, but consult your local salary laws to get some perspective. If the minimum wage in your city is $7.50 per hour, for example, it's probably reasonable to ask for anything between $5 and $12 for a babysitting job. It may be helpful to check out the United States Department of Labor site, dol.gov.

3. **The job expectations.** It's reasonable to charge parents more for additional responsibilities. For example, you could request $12 an hour for one child, $14 an hour for two, and so on. You may also be able to charge more than your usual rate for babysitting kids who require more care, like wheelchair-bound children. You should expect a bit of housework, like cleaning the dishes or cleaning up messes. But if the parents are asking you to go above and beyond, like mowing the lawn or mopping the floors, you should consider asking for more money.

4. **When to negotiate.** If an employer offers you an unreasonably low rate, you may be able to negotiate. And if you've worked with a family for a long time, they may be

TALES FROM THE CRIB

It was my first babysitting job and I was a timid sixth grader. I was hired by a family friend's mother. As I was young and new to babysitting, she asked me to watch the kids at a dinner party she was throwing. She said it shouldn't be too many kids and didn't mention the age range.

When I showed up on time for duty, there were fifteen kids, ages three to ten, and a specific limited set of boundaries they could play in—two bedrooms. Terrified, I attempted to corral the little demons together. One was jumping from the top bunk of a bunk bed onto a beanie bag chair, while another sent Hot Wheels cars flying across the room. One was crying because she didn't get the Barbie she wanted as another took out every single board game available and threw around Monopoly money and the pink and blue people from LIFE. I guess you could say I had my hands full. As the three hours became four hours and the evening drudged on, my limbs became numb. I struggled to clean up the huge mess that was made by what one would think was a tornado, while counting heads every minute.

And the funniest part? When I was officially done and on my way out the door, I was handed a twenty-dollar bill: $5 per hour for four hours with fifteen kids. Let's just say that that night might have shaved a few years off my life.

—Annika, fourteen

willing to give you a raise. Negotiating can be nerve-racking, but if you ask nicely and have convincing arguments, it might work. Here are some good arguments:

- The pay is not equal to my experience.
- The job has more responsibilities than the rate accounts for.
- I've been working here for a very long time, and I'd like to stay.
- The wage is way below the standard minimum wage.

19.

Knowing Your Rights and Obligations

Most jobs offer a clear course of action for legal issues. For instance, a newspaper reporter can go to the human resources department to report sexual harassment. Or a doctor can go to the hospital's accounting department to complain about a missing paycheck. Babysitters, on the other hand, are working directly with parents in a home setting.

And sometimes the rules aren't so obvious. But there are rules. Below are some ways to protect yourself from any issues and make sure you're following best practices too. These aren't all necessarily legal rights, but they are reasonable expectations in a respectful employer-employee relationship.

Your Rights

1. **The right to a clear job description.** Parents should clearly outline the important details of the job, like the pay, the number of hours, and the number of days (if more than one) that you've agreed to work. The parents should also tell you what responsibilities you should expect, like picking up the kids from school, orchestrating a playdate, or cooking dinner. It's even better if the parents send these details in an email. That way, you'll have the job description in writing in case there is any confusion later.

2. **The right to petty cash.** You should never have to pay for job expenses with your own money. If the kids are hungry, you shouldn't pay for groceries or takeout. If you drive the kids to school, you shouldn't have to pay for the gas, unless it's included in your salary. In general, the parents should leave you with cash for these things, or at the very least, reimburse you at the end of the evening. If they forget to include the money with your regular pay, kindly let them know what you needed to buy while they were out, and how much it cost. Keep all of your receipts as proof.

3. **The right to a safe environment**. A broken staircase, the presence of toxic chemicals like pesticides or secondhand smoke, or major fire hazards like loose electric wires in a garage full of paper are all things you shouldn't have to deal with on a job. If the situation can be easily fixed, ask the parents to take care of it before you

start working there. But if you think someone could get hurt, talk to an adult you trust about filing a complaint at your local health department. Of course, if there's a medical emergency or some criminal activity going on, you should call 911 right away!

4. **The right to a healthy environment, mentally.** Your employers must treat you with respect. They must value your time and your humanity. They must never harass you; act inappropriately; disrespect your race, religion, or gender identity; deny your pay; or treat you as though you're subhuman. They should never ask you to do things that are obviously beyond your pay grade or your abilities. They must maintain the boundaries of grown-up and babysitting teen at all times. If these boundaries are being breached, it is not your fault. Unfortunately, abusive workplace situations happen sometimes. Don't be afraid to tell a trusted adult about what's been going on. Of course, kids are a different matter—sometimes kids act very disrespectfully and inappropriately. But often that's a matter of maturity and development, and you are the more mature and responsible one in that situation.

5. **The right to quit.** If a job is not living up to your expectations, you have the right to quit. Obviously, you can't walk out on the kids while their parents are out. However, you can choose to not work for the family again. If you've already agreed to work for them long-term, it's common courtesy to give them enough time to find a replacement. Better yet, recommend a replacement to save

them time. Be polite. Don't ghost. You never know when you'll see someone again. (See page 129 for more tips on quitting the job.)

Your Obligations

1. **To uphold your end of the deal.** Like your employer, you are also responsible for doing whatever it is you agreed to do. This is not only a good business practice, but you can also get ghosted if you don't uphold your end of the deal. So make sure you don't promise to do something if you know you can't deliver.

2. **To keep the kids safe.** As soon as the parents leave the house, you are in charge of the children's physical wellbeing. You won't be arrested if they trip and fall, but there are ways to get in serious legal trouble. If you bypass your duties as a babysitter and the child is injured as a result, the parents can potentially sue you for negligence. For instance, if the child gets seriously hurt and you do nothing to help or if you throw a party at the parents' house without permission and someone lights the place on fire with an e-cig, you could be charged with negligence or property damage. Here are some more important ground rules:

   - Don't show up intoxicated.
   - Don't invite guests into the house.
   - Don't take your eyes off little kids.
   - Always call 911 in case of an emergency.

3. **To pay your taxes.** In IRS land, babysitters are considered self-employed childcare providers, and they have to pay taxes. If you make more than $400 in a year, you have to file a tax return using Form 1040. Typically, these jobs are "under the table," which means the IRS won't have been notified about this income—but if you don't report this income, you could get nabbed down the line and charged a bunch of money. Head to IRS.gov and read about self-employment taxes for more information.

20.

Updating the Parents

When the kids' parents come home, you're still in business mode. Even though you're covered in food and a bit disheveled, your professionalism is still on trial. The few minutes after the parents arrive is your chance to show off your skills, prove that you're trustworthy, improve your performance, and maybe land more babysitting gigs. Once the parents have had a chance to settle in and check on their kids, wrap things up with these best practices.

Give Them the Good Stuff

Tell the parents all the great things you accomplished. Did you cook dinner, invent a game, or put the kids to bed? Say so. Parents will be happy to know that they can trust you with these tasks.

Give Them the Not-So-Good Stuff

Tell the parents about any loose ends. Apologize for leaving dirty dishes. Explain if the kids refused to eat their vegetables. Show them the vase that broke during an unruly round of hide-and-seek. Good babysitting bosses will respect your honesty and may be able to offer advice for the future.

Show Off Your Bond

If the kids are awake, this could be a great opportunity to show off your new connection with them. Involve them in a conversation in front of their parents. Ask them if they loved the green eggs and ham you made. Keep it light and funny. And remember to give them a friendly goodbye.

Ask Outstanding Questions

You'll probably have tons of questions when the parents come home. Is little Suzy's jaw clicking normal? Do you use baby powder? Does the backyard light always flicker like that? This is the time to get answers to anything you were wondering about while you were on the job. And parents will likely appreciate your concern.

Handle Payments Efficiently

Do the math. Make sure the parents give you the correct amount for your wages and expenses. For extra assurance, you can type up an invoice with all your expense receipts attached. If they accidentally underpay you, politely inform them. If they overpay, you should give the extra money back. Hard as this may be, it will prove that you have excellent character.

SAFETY FIRST!

Q. How do I get home?

A. The most important thing is that you're safe. That should be your priority, the parents' priority, and the priority of your parents or guardians too. Unless you live within walking distance in a very safe neighborhood, you should arrange a ride or escort in advance. Don't just expect a ride from your babysitting bosses unless you've already agreed on something. But if you're stranded without a ride and they seem completely unconcerned and unhelpful, you may need to outright demand an Uber ride home or call a trusted adult.

21.
Keeping and Quitting a Job

You're finally home. You've survived a successful babysitting gig and had fun while you were at it. You breathe easy knowing that you aren't totally responsible for little lives for a while. Is it over? Not if you want to be invited back. Alternatively, maybe it didn't go as well as you expected. The kids were crazy. You tried your best, but it felt as though it wasn't a good fit. There are things you should do if you want to keep or quit a job while still being professional.

Keeping a Job

To look like a pro even when you're off the clock, follow up each gig with a thank-you and a brief recap. The recap is a brief courtesy text (or email) letting the parents know that you really enjoyed your babysitting experience. You can also mention some of the fun things you did with the kids. It's a great way to seem eager for more work. Here's a sample recap that you can use as a model for your own:

> *Hello [insert parent's name],*
>
> *I just wanted to let you know that I really enjoyed my time with Johnny and Katie. No kid has ever beaten me at checkers before. You really have a wonderful family. Thanks so much for the opportunity! I hope to see them again soon.*

Parents are busy, and they often take a while to respond. Sometimes there's not much more you can do except cross your fingers and hope for a call back. But if after a couple of weeks you still haven't heard from them about a possible next time, try some friendly prodding like this:

> *Hello [insert parent's name],*
>
> *I wanted to check in and see if you'll need my services next week or later on. I had a great time with the family, and I wanted to see if I should make some room for you in my schedule. I look forward to hearing from you!*

If the parents hire you back, respond immediately with a thank-you. But if the parents give you the cold shoulder or tell you (nicely) that they won't need your services, try not to stress out. One rejection doesn't mean you can't babysit for other families. Mourn the loss for a few days, and be sure to handle any rejection with grace. You never know if the parents will change their minds. And you still want them to like you enough to recommend you to other families.

Here's a sample professional response to a rejection:

Thank you for letting me know. While I'm disappointed, I'm glad I had the opportunity to meet your children. Please contact me any time if you change your mind in the future.

Quitting a Job

Maybe your first time working with a family was enough. Or maybe you've given it a few tries, and things aren't quite working out. Quitting a job is hard, especially when kids are involved. But you shouldn't stick around out of guilt. And you shouldn't just end things without offering an explanation. Quitting is a lot like breaking up with a significant other. There's a nice way to do it.

Gather your reasons. People quit their jobs for a wide range of reasons, so you should have a reason too. Take time to think about why you're unhappy with the job. You may or may not share all of these reasons with the family, but you'll have them in your back pocket. These are some reasons:

- You feel unsafe.
- It doesn't pay enough, and you can't negotiate with the parents.

- You don't have time to continue.
- You got another job.
- You're moving far away.

Let them down gently. You can give the parents your reasons without being harsh. Give them plenty of notice so they have time to find a replacement. For instance, if you want to quit because you can't stand their kids, write something polite like this:

> *Hello [insert parent's name],*
>
> *I'm deeply sorry, but I'm afraid that I can no longer babysit for Lucas. I'm feeling quite overwhelmed by the job and don't think it's a great fit. If you'd like, I can babysit for the next two weeks while you find somebody new.*

Refer someone you trust. If you can, recommend a trusted, qualified friend or acquaintance for the job (but be sure to tell your friend your reason for quitting the job). This shows the parents that you care about the job (and the kids' well-being) even if you are quitting. It's often hard to find a replacement sitter right away, so parents will appreciate the help. Be sure not to send your friend into a bad or dangerous situation.

Ask for a recommendation. If you left your babysitting job on good terms, keep in touch with the parents so they'll be willing to recommend you to other parents. One good way to keep in touch is to email the parents once in a while and ask about the children. Or stop by occasionally for a visit (if it's appropriate). This will keep you fresh in the parents' minds so they can give you an excellent reference.

TALES FROM THE CRIB

While taking care of a young boy, I was . . . bitten. Not a little, light, bite. A hard, abrasive bite on the leg. The boy liked to pretend he was a dinosaur and while I could handle the roaring and running around, I was hardly prepared to be bitten! Here's what happened: I was taking care of the other children when I felt a tremendous pain in my leg. Much to my surprise, when I turned around the little "dinosaur" boy was staring up at me innocently. With his dinosaur-like bite he had accidentally ripped through my jeans and even punctured my skin! I couldn't believe that such a little boy had bitten me with such power!

—Erin, fifteen

22.
Taking Things Further

Are you thinking bigger? Since you've racked up all these childcare qualifications, maybe you don't feel like going the traditional babysitting route anymore. If you're still serious about babysitting, but you want to take it further and make more money, you have lots of options.

Promote Yourself

Put yourself out there with advertising. It will help you garner clients, local buzz, and maybe even babysitting club members. These days, anyone can advertise with some pretty low-price methods.

Business cards. Business cards pack all of your contact information onto professional, wallet-size documents. Business cards are great for subtle advertising during conversations. If you overhear that your friend's parents are looking for a babysitter later on, you can hand them your swanky-looking card for future reference. Or if you overhear a mother complaining about the lack of babysitters in town, hand her a card to prove her wrong. You can also give your cards to

your current clients to hand out to their friends and associates.

Posters or flyers. If you live in a safe, intimate community, you can post flyers that advertise your skills. Flyers are one-page, informal advertisements that you can post around town. They're cheap to make and fun to post, and maybe your dream employer will see your flyer and hire you. Be sure to post them in family-friendly locations where parents are likely to go, like restaurants, grocery stores, or libraries.

Social Media or Online

In the beginning of your babysitting career, you will get most gigs through word-of-mouth. If you have more experience, you might consider using social media, a personal website, and a newsletter e-blast to advertise your babysitting services. Perhaps one day you can host a YouTube channel with your babysitting tips. But first things first. Babysitting usually starts as a few hours a week before it becomes a 24-7 influencer gig.

Team Up with Other Sitters

Teaming up with other babysitters is a great way to get lots of jobs without shouldering all the work. You'll have help hunting for and taking jobs, and you won't be responsible for maintaining the business all on your own. You'll also be able to hang out with friends and voice your problems to people who understand.

Starting a club. To start a club, get dependable people working with you. Preferably, they should have plenty of babysitting experience and maybe some experience with websites, advertising, or money management. Together, you can take turns garnering jobs, taking jobs, answering phones, running meetings, collecting dues, making the popcorn—however you choose to run things!

Starting an online babysitting group.

If you don't have time for in-person meetings but you want to meet other sitters, you could start an online babysitting group. You could moderate a Facebook page, a personal website, or a blog forum where local babysitters can ask questions, post jobs, give advice, and build a community. If you get a good response, maybe this could lead to a bona fide club.

Look into Other Jobs That Use Your Skills

If you love childcare but you don't want anything to do with babysitting anymore, you can use your qualifications to climb the ladder and apply for other jobs. (Some of them may pay more money too.) If you want to take your babysitting skills further, these are some jobs you can consider:

Camp counselor. Overnight or day camp counselors are in charge of multiple kids, sometimes for an entire summer. Some camps have entry-level junior counseling positions for teenagers.

Tutoring. If you've done any babysitting for school-age kids, you've probably already done some level of tutoring. If you like tutoring, why not pursue it? Bone up on your subjects. You can even earn certifications to teach the ins and outs of standardized tests like the PSAT.

Local kids' spaces. Do you just like the "play" part of babysitting? You may be interested in working for a kids' birthday party service or at a local kid-friendly space. You can try working as a clown, a magician, an adventure associate at a local campground, a ticket taker at a local carnival, a gymnastics coach assistant, a children's song musician, an arts-and-crafts organizer, or more.

Internships. If you're seriously interested in a childcare or an education career path, look for an internship in your chosen field. Maybe you can intern in a school, a day-care site, or a social work agency. Unfortunately, internships are usually low paying or, at certain nonprofits, unpaid, but you get unprecedented learning experiences, references, and a new shining star on your résumé.

Congratulations! You're on your way to becoming a star sitter. Get out there and work! And don't forget to bring this handy guide with you—just in case.

RESOURCES

Basic Training

Mayo Clinic
> https://www.mayoclinic.com
> The Mayo Clinic provides extensive and reliable medical information. From diaper rash to the flu, this site offers step-by-step instructions on how to recognize and handle illnesses. It also has information for handling tantrums.

Parents
> https://www.parents.com
> Learn from the experts! Parents magazine always comes with great advice for childcare, including new recipe ideas, sleep issues, and fun holiday activities.

US Department of Labor
> https://www.dol.gov
> If you're curious about things like minimum wage laws, babysitters' rights, how many people are babysitting or nannying in the world, the US Department of Labor is your best bet for accurate stats.

In Case of Emergency

Poison Control Center
> https://www.poison.org
> 800-222-1222
> If a child has ingested something toxic, call a poison control center immediately. Learn a jingle to commit it to memory at https://www.poison.org/jingle.

Red Cross First Aid-CPR-AED
> https://www.redcross.org/take-a-class
> The Red Cross is the most reliable organization for learning first aid and CPR. Get certified—it'll look great on your résumé!

Edutainment

Highlights Kids

https://www.highlightskids.com/

Kids and sitters alike can discover craft and recipe ideas, jokes, games, puzzles, and cool science on this site.

Khan Academy

https://www.khanacademy.org

When kids need homework help, Khan Academy can be a great way to access free online video lessons in every subject, at every level.

KidsHealth

https://www.kidshealth.org/kid/recipes

This nonprofit, expert site is not only an excellent source for information on illness, but it also has kid-friendly recipes! The site also includes recipe ideas for kids who are vegetarian, diabetic, or lactose intolerant.

Kids Know It

http://gws.ala.org/content/kids-know-it-network

This educational site for kids is full of astronomy, biology, dinosaur, geography, history, math, memory, and spelling games. It's a great resource for babysitters with kids who want internet time.

PBS Kids

https://www.pbskids.org

PBS Kids offers quality, educational games for kids ages three to eight. And you might have fun recognizing the characters from your childhood!

Scholastic Homework Help

https://www.scholastic.com/parents/school-success/school
-success-guides/homework-help.html

Is the child getting frustrated with homework? Scholastic offers free online help for parents and caretakers. The webpage has interesting articles, research tips, and study techniques in every subject.

Sesame Street Family Play App
From the brilliant minds of Sesame Street, the Family Play app offers more than 130 real world games to play all over the house. Kids can keep busy, move their bodies, or calm down using specifically tailored games. Available on all devices.

Sittercity's Compendium of Extraordinary Knowledge
https://www.sittercity.com
Sittercity is a widely respected babysitting job site, but you need to be eighteen to join. However, you can still benefit from Sittercity's wisdom. The site has loads of ideas for babysitting activities, from bubble print pop art to making faces on pancakes.

INDEX

ABOUT THE AUTHOR

Halley Bondy is a professional freelance writer, journalist, editor, producer, and mom based in Brooklyn. You can find her work in NBC News, Scary Mommy, The Balance, Contently, Digital Trends, Bustle, Romper, The Outline, MTV, and more. She writes scripts for the *Masters of Scale* podcast, and has written for *You Must Remember This*. She has written three other books for Zest including *Speak Up! A Guide to Having a Say and Speaking Your Mind*.

photo by Heather White